COL MAC 5.50

THE NATURAL
SUPERIORITY OF WOMEN

THE
NATURAL
SUPERIORITY
OF WOMEN

Ashley Montagu

NEW REVISED EDITION

COLLIER BOOKS
A Division of Macmillan Publishing Co., Inc.
New York

COLLIER MACMILLAN PUBLISHERS
London

GRATEFUL ACKNOWLEDGMENT IS MADE TO THE FOLLOWING PUBLISHERS
FOR PERMISSION TO QUOTE FROM THE BOOKS MENTIONED:

Appleton-Century-Crofts, Inc., *The Study of Man*, by Ralph Linton.
Copyright, 1936, by D. Appleton-Century Co., Inc.

Coward-McCann, Inc., *Music and Women*, by Sophie Drinker.
Copyright, 1948, by Sophie Drinker.

Greenberg, *The Sex Life of the American Woman*, edited by Albert
Ellis. Copyright, 1953.

Grune & Stratton, Inc., *The Psychology of Women*, by Helene
Deutsch. Copyright, 1944, 1945, by Grune & Stratton, Inc.

Harcourt, Brace & Company, *Women and Men*, by Amram
Scheinfeld. Copyright, 1943, 1944, by Amram Scheinfeld.

The John Day Company, *Of Men and Women*, by Pearl S. Buck.
Copyright, 1941, by Pearl S. Buck.

Macmillan Publishing Co., Inc., *The Meaning of Intelligence*, by George
Stoddard. Copyright, 1943, by Macmillan Publishing Co., Inc.

Portions of this book first appeared in *The Saturday Review* and
in *The Saturday Evening Post*, copyright 1945 by The Curtis
Publishing Company.

Copyright © 1952, 1953, 1968, 1974 by Ashley Montagu

*Macmillan Publishing Co., Inc.
866 Third Avenue, New York, N.Y. 10022
Collier-Macmillan Canada Ltd.*

Library of Congress Cataloging in Publication Data

Montagu, Ashley, Date
   The natural superiority of women.

   Includes bibliographical references.
   1. Woman.   I. Title.   [DNLM: 1. Women.   HQ1206   A826n   1974]
HQ1206.M65   1974   301.41'2   73-8087
ISBN 0-02-096080-8

New Revised Edition

The Natural Superiority of Women is published in a hardcover
edition by Macmillan Publishing Co., Inc.

15   14   13   12   11   10   9   8   7   6

Printed in the United States of America

To *Marjorie*
With All My Love

Contents

Preface
to the First Edition

I HAVE BEEN THINKING about the theme of this book for some thirty years. For an equal number of years, I have discussed it, on and off, with various friends. However, it was not until I talked about my ideas with Norman Cousins, editor of the *Saturday Review*, that, upon his urging, I set them down in an article bearing the same title as this book. This was published in the March 1, 1952, issue of the *Saturday Review*.

Because it was Norman Cousins who suggested the writing of this book, it is a very real pleasure to be able to express my thanks to him both for his interest and for his enthusiasm. I am also obliged to Mr. Jack Cominsky, publisher of the *Saturday Review*, for many courtesies. Many thanks are due to Mrs. Marjorie Child Husted for her continued interest in this volume. It has been a pleasure to work with Mr. George Platt Brett, Jr., President of The Macmillan Company, and with my gentle editor, Miss Eleanor Daniels. To my wife I owe deepest thanks for her helpful readings of the manuscript, and for being all that a naturally superior person should be.

A. M.

Preface
to the Second Edition

SINCE THIS BOOK was first published in 1953 a great deal of new information has become available. The new material unexceptionally supports and confirms the conclusions of this book. These conclusions are based on incontrovertible evidence, evidence that can be confirmed by anyone who will take the trouble to examine it. The facts cannot be argued away. At most it is their interpretation that may be questioned. Here, in the light of the findings of science I have attempted to offer the most highly probable explanation of the meaning of the facts. I do not think that these explanations can be seriously challenged. It is necessary to make this unequivocally clear. This is not a work based on the author's opinions. What I am trying to say in this book is that the evidence set out in it represents the facts of nature. Anyone who desires to argue with the facts of nature should not be intimidated by such a statement. On the contrary, he should be encouraged to doubt and to question, for most people have a way of mistaking their prejudices for the laws of nature. I do not claim to be exempt from this particular frailty. None of us is. The facts set out in this book, however, are either true or false. If it can be shown that any of them are questionable, I would welcome the evidence. To my knowledge no one has thus far been able to produce such evidence.

I have endeavored to leave the book essentially as it was written, except that I have brought up to date, with the latest findings and figures available up to the time of publication, all the materials presented. I have also added a certain amount of new material. The results of recent research have in many places enabled me to present the earlier data in reinforced form.

If, for millennia, women have been the "inferior race" of the masculine world, their legitimate claims to being valued at their true worth can no longer be dismissed with a contemptuous shrug or with mordant humor consigned to the collection of more cranky notions entertained by women and their defenders. Prejudice and ignorance have too long complicated the relations between the sexes. The times call for greater understanding based on knowledge. I have, in this book, attempted to provide both.

The recent development of the women's liberation movement constitutes a happy augury for the future, for the liberation of women will mean also the liberation of men. Toward that end this book is offered as a modest contribution.

Princeton, New Jersey   A. M.
19 March 1968

Preface to the
New Revised Edition

FOR THIS THIRD EDITION a new chapter has been added, "The Sexual Superiority of Women," which first appeared under that title in *The Sex Life of the American Woman* edited by Albert Ellis and published by Greenberg in 1953. Additional material has been added throughout the book, and there has been a thorough revision and updating of the whole work.

I am most grateful for statistical help to the Women's Bureau of the U. S. Department of Labor. To Philip Gordon I owe many thanks for his careful reading of the proofs.

Princeton, N.J.   A. M.
September 1973

Foreword

THIS BOOK is designed to bring the sexes closer together, not to set them apart by placing one above the other. If in these pages the natural superiority of women is emphasized, it is because the fact has thus far received far too little attention, and the time is long overdue that both men and women become aware of it and fully understand its meaning. Natural superiority does not imply social inequality; on the other hand, the plea of this book is for more mutual love and understanding and complete social equality of the sexes. We must acquire a sense of values that will enhance the appreciation of the sexes for each other. As Tennyson wrote, "The woman's cause is man's. They rise or fall together."

That women are superior to men will probably be a new idea to most people. I am told that there have been two or three books that have made such a claim; but these, I gather, make the claim on grounds very different from those discussed in the present study; I regret to say that I haven't read them. In any event, I should like the present book to represent an independent contribution to the subject rather than an analysis or digest of the work of other people. Scott Nearing writes me that almost half a century ago he and Nellie Seeds published a book entitled *Woman and Social Progress* in which certain hitherto unallowed claims were made for women. It has also been pointed out to me that in 1917 H. L. Mencken published a book entitled *In Defense of Women*. Doubtless there have been other books on this theme, and doubtless they are good. In foregoing the pleasure of reading the works of others, I shall, I know, be voluntarily depriving both the reader and myself of a great many valuable supports and reenforcements that would have made this book stronger than it is. I have, of course, read a fair number of books on women and the sexes, and there can be not the least doubt that much of what I have read in this field has become part of me and that I have reproduced ideas whose paternity is not my own. I am deeply grateful to all my teachers and predecessors, even though I may no longer be able to recall many by name or credit them with ideas derived from them.

Finally, do let us preserve our sense of humor and of balance. If sometimes I poke a little lighthearted fun at my own sex, I hope no man will be humorless enough to think that I am casting aspersions upon him.

A. M.

If ever the world sees a time when women shall come together purely and simply for the benefit and good of mankind, it will be a power such as the world has never known.

—Matthew Arnold

If I were asked . . . to what the singular prosperity and growing strength of that people ought mainly to be attributed, I should reply: To the superiority of their women.

—Democracy in America, PT. II, BK. III, CH. 12, 1840
Alexis De Tocqueville

Adams owed more to the American woman than to all the American men he ever heard of, and felt not the smallest call to defend his sex who seemed able to take care of themselves; but from the point of view of sex he felt much curiosity to know how far the woman was right, and, in pursuing this inquiry, he caught the trick of affirming that the woman was the superior. Apart from truth, he owed her at least that compliment.

—The Education of Henry Adams, CHAPTER XXX

THE NATURAL
SUPERIORITY OF WOMEN

1.

The Natural
Superiority of Women

"OH, NO!" I can hear it said, "*not* superior. Equal, partners, complementary, different, but *not* superior. What an idea!" Men will mostly smile, while women, alarmed, will rush to the defense of men—as women always have and always will. I hope that what I shall have to say in this book will make them even more willing to do so, for men need their help more than they know.

Certainly there have been people who have cogently, if not altogether convincingly, argued that women were as good as men; but I do not know, nor have I read, of anyone who has provided the evidence that women are better than, or superior to, men. How, indeed, could one successfully argue such a case in the face of all the evidence to the contrary? Is it not a fact that by far the largest number of geniuses, painters, poets, philosophers, scientists, and so on, have been men, and that women have made, by comparison, a very poor showing? Clearly the superiority is with men. Where are the Leonardos, the Michelangelos, the Shakespeares, the Donnes, the Galileos, the Bachs, the Mozarts, the Kants, and the Whiteheads of the feminine world? In fields in which women have excelled, in poetry and the novel, how many poets and novelists of truly first rank have there been? Haven't well-bred young women been educated for centuries in music? And how many among them have been great composers or instrumentalists? Of composers—none of the first rank. Among instrumentalists—there have been such accomplished artists as Myra Hess and Wanda Landowska. Possibly there is a clue here in answer to the question asked. May it not be that women are just about to emerge from the period of subjection during which they were the menials of the masculine world?

Almost everywhere women are achieving positions that were once considered beyond their capacity. The most exclusive scientific societies have at last opened their doors and admitted women to the highest honors which it is within their power to bestow. Fifty years ago it was considered inconceivable that any woman would ever have brains enough to attain great distinction in science. Mme. Curie was regarded as a sort of rare mutation, the exception that proved the rule of masculine superiority. But the contemporary women members of the most distinguished scientific societies are no longer "exceptions." Nor is Lise Meitner, of Uranium 238 fame, an exception. And Mme. Curie no longer remains the only woman to share in the Nobel Prize award for science. There is Marie Curie's daughter, Irène Curie-Joliot, and there is Gerty Cori, who was awarded the Nobel Prize for physiology and medicine in 1947. Marie Curie was the first scientist to receive the Nobel Prize twice for distinguished scientific achievement. Originally she received the Prize together with her husband in physics in 1903, and alone in chemistry in 1911. In 1963 Maria Goeppert-Mayer shared the Nobel Prize for physics, and in 1964 Dorothy Hodgkin was awarded the Prize in chemistry. There is also the discoverer of the eighty-seventh element, francium, Marguerite Perey, who, in March, 1962, was the first woman to be elected a member of the French Academy of Sciences. Nobel Prizes in literature have gone to Selma Lagerlöf, Grazia Deledda, Sigrid Undset, Pearl Buck, and Gabriela Mistral. As an artist Mary Cassatt was every bit as good as her great French friends Degas and Manet considered her to be, but it has taken the rest of the world another fifty years grudgingly to admit it. Among contemporary artists Georgia O'Keeffe can hold her own with the best.

However, it is not going to be any part of this book to show that women are about to emerge as superior scientists, musicians, painters, or the like. I believe that in these fields they may emerge with abilities equal to those of men but possibly not in as great numbers, largely because the motivations and aspirations of most women will continue to be directed elsewhere. What must be pointed out is that women are just beginning to emerge from their long and unjustified period of subjection.

It may be of interest to recall here, as illustrative of the prevailing traditional attitudes toward women, that the entire article on women in the first edition of the *Encyclopaedia Britannica,* published in 1771, consisted of the six words, "The Female of man. See *Homo.*" In the politics of sex most men have been Tories.

If there is any man who without blushing can contemplate the history of his sex's conduct toward women, let it in charity be set down to the fact that he very likely does not consider himself responsible for the errors of his predecessors. Thus absolved from all responsibility for the past, it may be hoped that he will henceforth conduct himself with more intelligence and a greater sense of responsibility. The women of the nineteenth century were treated in a manner not unlike that which is still the bitter experience of the Black in many parts of the world. Traits that are mythically attributed to the Black at the present time were for many generations saddled upon women, the second-class citizens of a patriarchal society. Women, it was alleged, had smaller brains than men, and less intelligence; they were more emotional and unstable; in a crisis you could always depend upon them to swoon or become otherwise helpless; they were weak and sickly creatures; they had little judgment and less sense; they could not be entrusted with the handling of money; and as for the world outside, there they could be employed only at the most menial and routine tasks.

The most effective demolition of this series of myths occurred during World War I, when for the first time women were called upon to replace men in occupations that were formerly the exclusive preserve of men. They became bus drivers, conductors, factory workers, farm workers, laborers, supervisors, executive officers, and a great many other things at which many had believed they could not work. At first it was said they didn't do as well as men; then it was grudgingly admitted that they weren't so bad; and by the time the war was over many employers were reluctant to exchange their women employees for men! But the truth was out: women could do as well as men in most of the fields that had been considered forever closed to them because of their alleged natural incapacities; and in many fields, particularly where delicate precision work was involved, they had proved themselves superior to men. For women the period from 1918 to 1939 was essentially one of consolidation of gains, so that by the time World War II broke out there was no hesitation on the part of anyone in calling women to serve in the civilian roles of men and in many cases in the armed services.

But women have yet some distance to go before they achieve full emancipation. When men speak of the "Rights of Man," they mean the rights of men—men who will attend to the rights of everyone else. Alas, they have been singularly slow to establish the rights of women; and I am not speaking simply of political rights: I mean all the rights to which a human being, by virtue of his being a human being, should be heir. But since I have mentioned political rights, consider how appalling it is that as late as 1945, when the U.N. Charter was signed, that there were only thirty-six countries in the whole world which accorded women full political rights. In the United States, in so many ways one of the most progressive lands in the world, the only right guaranteed American women by the Constitution is the right to vote, and this by an amendment, the Nineteenth, passed in 1919 and largely the work of Susan B. Anthony. Of all other rights—such as equal protection under the law, the right to jury service, the right to control income and earnings, the right to make contracts, the right to enter any business or profession, the right not to be deprived of one's property without due process of law, the right to choose unrestrictedly the hours of work, the right to custody of children, to divorce or freedom of speech —of all these rights none is constitutionally guaranteed to women; they are states' rights, which are at the disposition of state legislatures, and may be changed as the wind listeth.

The Equal Rights Amendment to the Constitution has been an election-year promise both by the Democratic and by the Republican parties on several occasions, but it has yet to be enacted into law. The proposed Amendment reads: "Equality under the law shall not be denied or abridged by the United States or by any state on account of sex." Even at this late date this proposed Amendment has not yet become part of the Constitution of the United States. In 1948 a Senate Judiciary Subcommittee recommended, by a vote of seven to one, that the Amendment "do pass." But no further action was taken. In 1972 the Amendment was passed and went to the states for ratification.

Apart from the right to vote, American women have no more constitutional rights than they had in 1789; in other words, medieval English common law is the law that still governs women and places upon them the stigma of inferiority and bondage. Is it too much to expect that full constitutional legal equality for women in the United States is now a matter of a very short time? The constitutional and legal recognition of the equality of the sexes will be an important step in the right direction, but it will become part of the American Constitution only if enough citizens are in favor of it to make themselves effectively heard. However, this does not mean that the relationships between the sexes will thus become automatically and intelligently balanced. Such recognition will help; but the basic, age-old problems between the sexes will no more be solved by constitutional Amendment than have the much younger racial and religious problems. These difficulties are all problems in human relations, and until they are solved, human beings will in large numbers continue to behave inefficiently and unintelligently.

Women have been conditioned to believe that they are inferior to men, and they have assumed that what everyone believes is a fact of nature. Because men occupy the superior positions in almost all societies, such superiority is taken to be a natural one. "Woman's place is in the home," and man's place is in the countinghouse and on the board of directors. "Women should not meddle in men's affairs." And yet the world does move. Women are entering the countinghouses and are being seated as members of the boards of directors of large corporations. In the United States women have become members of Congress and have even attained Cabinet rank; in many other parts of the world, in even greater numbers, women have attained similar positions. They have participated in peace conferences, in the Assembly of the United Nations, and in international organizations of many different kinds. "Nevertheless," I wrote in the first edition of this book early in 1953, "it is still incon- ceivable to many persons that there should ever be a woman President or Prime Minister. And yet that day, too, will come. *Eppur si muove!*"

Indeed, the world does move. In September of that very same year, 1953, the Eighth Assembly of the United Nations elected its first woman President, Mme. Vijaya Laksmi Pandit of India. In 1960 Mrs. Sirimavo Bandaranaike became Prime Minister of Ceylon, the first woman in the world to hold such an office. In January, 1966, Mrs. Indira Gandhi was sworn in as Prime Minister of India. In March, 1969, Mrs. Golda Meir was elected Prime Minister of Israel.

It is curious, is it not, that we should so readily accept the reality of a queen-ruler, while our hackles rise at the very thought of a woman President? Queen Elizabeth I of England has been a heroine of the English-speaking world for five centuries, and Queen Elizabeth II of England is today one of the most popular figures of the English-speaking world. So is Queen Juliana of the Netherlands. Queen Jadwiga (1373–99) of Poland is remembered as one of its greatest rulers and one of the truly inspired peacemakers of history. In an age of bloodshed and cruelty, she consistently tried to settle internal and international conflicts and resist aggression by diplomacy, arbitration, negotiation, and appeals to reason and justice. Believing in education as a basis for enlightenment, she left her jewels to endow the University of Kracow. Queen Elizabeth I and Queen Victoria rank among the greatest of English monarchs, and their reigns coincided with a rise in prestige and prosperity such as England had never seen; yet many Englishmen would still balk as much at *electing* a queen to rule over them (even though she ruled only in name as a constitutional monarch) as many Americans would at electing a woman President. It is, however, important to observe that today there is probably a higher proportion of people who would vote for a woman President than there has been at any other time in our history, and that is a healthy sign.

Having successfully freed herself from her thralldom to man, woman has now to emancipate herself from the myth of inferiority and to realize her potentialities to the fullest.

How, it was asked earlier, can one argue the natural superiority of women in the face of all the evidence to the contrary? The evidence to the contrary merits our serious attention, and that it shall receive. What has, up to now, usually been omitted from discussions of this sort is the evidence in favor of the natural superiority of women, that is, her biological superiority. I shall set out the evidence in this book.

As we shall see, the findings of modern science controvert the age-old belief in feminine inferiority. It is not only possible to show that most of the things that have been said about women to their disadvantage are false; it is also possible to show that women are actually better endowed than men. Women, on the whole, have a greater number of biological advantages than men, but for the most part they have not been permitted to enjoy them. When myths grow hoary with age, they are frequently accepted as truths. The myths about women have been accepted as truths by both sexes from time immemorial, and custom and rationalization have helped to keep them alive. The seventeenth-century French philosopher, La Barre, writing on this subject, said, "Men persuade themselves of very many things, for which they can give no Reason; because their Assurance is founded upon slight Appearances, by which they suffer themselves to be hurried: and would have as strongly believed the contrary, if the Impressions of Sense or Custom had thereto determined them after the same manner." Quite so, but the fact is that men have always been able to provide reasons for their beliefs in feminine inferiority. Wasn't it *obvious* that women were inferior to men? Yes and no, for what is obvious is not necessarily so for the reasons we are inclined to favor; on the other hand, our "reasons" are often nothing but rationalizations, devices for believing what we want to believe, for *reasons*—most of the time—not clearly known to ourselves. The first of the great feminists understood this quite clearly: Mary Wollstonecraft, in her *A Vindication of the Rights of Woman* (1792), wrote, "Men, in general, seem to employ their reason to justify prejudices, which they have imbibed, they cannot trace how, rather than root them out."

Most women will not like this talk of "superiority" and "inferiority" any more than I do. We have had altogether too much of these terms in the recent past in connection with so-called "superior" and "inferior" races; the unspeakable horrors that have been committed in the name of such pathogenic ideas constitute the blackest mark in the history of mankind. I should not have written this book had I thought there was any danger that women would adopt "superior" airs and deal with men as their "inferiors." Most women have much better sense than that. The one thing we may be certain women will never do is to lord it over men as men have for so long lorded it over them. The truly superior person doesn't need to lord it over anyone; it is only the inferior person who, in order to feel that he is superior, must have someone to look down on. The genuinely superior person looks neither up nor down: he looks straight at you.

Men are both numerically and biologically a "minority group," while women are both numerically and biologically a "superior group." One need not emphasize, therefore, the peculiar necessity of generosity toward the "minority group." The greatest victory one can yield to one's traditional enemy is to become like him.

In this book I propose to bring some of our rationalizations and the reasons for them into the light of day for everyone to see plainly and clearly, to make the relevant *facts* available about both sexes—facts that are all too little known and all too seldom discussed. With the facts thus placed at his disposal, as well as the conclusions to be drawn from them, it is to be hoped that the reader will rethink the foundations of his beliefs concerning feminine inferiority and not permit himself to be deflected from the truth by prejudice and entrenched traditional beliefs. The truth will make men free as well as women, for until women are freed from the myths that at present impede their progress, no man can be free or mentally completely healthy. The liberation of woman means the liberation of man. As Richard Garnett put it many years ago, "Man and Woman may only enter Paradise hand in hand. Together, the myth tells us, they left it and together they must return."

2.

The Subjection
of Women

WHY IS IT THAT in most of the cultures of which we
have any knowledge, women are considered to be
a sort of lower being, a creature human enough but not
quite so human as the male; certainly not as wise, not as
intelligent; and lacking in most of the capacities and
abilities with which the male is so plentifully endowed?

How has it come about that women have occupied a
position of subjection to men in almost all the cultures of
which we have any knowledge?

Mankind is several million years old. So is womankind. Since we know practically nothing directly about
the social life of our early ancestors, the following discussion must, to a large extent, be conjectural. But if,
with all the necessary qualifications of caution, we were
to judge from what we know of the social life of existing
nonliterate (often miscalled "primitive peoples"), we
should have to conclude that for the greater part of the
several million years men have, on the whole, been dic-
tatorial, unfair, and quite unkind to women. During
their long period of subjection, women have been treated
as chattels, slaves, housekeepers, economic advantages,

and sexual conveniences; indeed, throughout a great part of the world they are still so treated.

How did this relationship between the sexes come about?

There are certain biological facts of pertinence here— I should say not the biological facts so much as the interpretations that have been given to them. Because women bear children and nurse them, they are forced to be much more sedentary than men. Woman is the cricket on the hearth; man is the eagle on the wing. Women stay at home to nurse and care for their children, to prepare food. Men leave the hearth for the hunt.

It is necessary to understand that throughout more than nine-tenths of the long history of mankind, its economy was characterized by food-gathering and hunting. Agriculture and herding of animals were unknown; habitations were the mouths of caves or the most primitive kind of windbreaks, similar, no doubt, to those built by the Australian aborigines of the present day. Tools were mostly of stone, and implements were of the simplest kind, and few. Spears, hand hammers, choppers, grating and cutting tools of stone had been invented, as well as a fair number of other implements useful in the chase and for domestic purposes; but such equipment did not make hunting easy. Women could use their hand implements for the digging of tubers and other root plants, but men required implements that would travel some distance to reach and slay the hunted animal. Often a man would have to travel many miles in order to secure his prey; sometimes he might be away for days, even weeks. His mate generally remained on home grounds.

Now, step by step, let us consider the consequences of the different roles played by each of the sexes, roles arising from the fundamental biological sexual differences relating to reproduction, always remembering that we are discussing the roles of the sexes during the long phase of man's food-gathering and hunting stage of development.

First, the female is rendered sedentary, even though before becoming a mother she may have been as mobile as any man or boy. Thus her experience becomes limited to her domestic duties, and she is confined to her home territory. She is the food-gatherer; her husband is the hunter. Her task will be to gather plants and tubers, honey, grubs, and the like; in short, whatever is edible and can be procured without hunting. Between caring for her children, food-gathering, preparing meals, and performing other domestic activities, little time is left her for any other kind of experience.

The male, on the other hand, while he may be quite highly domesticated, is nevertheless called upon to exercise his ingenuity very much more frequently, and in a more varied manner, than the female. As a consequence of his hunting activities, he acquires a great deal of the kind of experience that almost never falls to the lot of the female. He learns to read tracks and signs of the presence of animals or men; he becomes something of a naturalist, for it is important to him to be able to distinguish between what is edible and what is not; he learns a great deal about the habits and ways of animal and plant life, about the weather, and about the rocks and other materials from which his implements will be made, and numerous other details associated with a hunting economy. Because he is the hunter, he knows best what implements serve him most effectively in the hunt, and it is he who is the inventor and maker of hunting implements. He develops skill in the use of hunting and accessory implements, and he transfers his skill to the making of articles of domestic use; when he has time he may decorate them with designs of magical and religious significance. Out of these occupations, in later stages of cultural development, such designs may be elaborated and put into nonobjective, abstract forms, or into purely representational forms. Though men may have given rise to the growth of art in this way, it cannot be doubted that where pottery decoration and weaving and, later, basket making are concerned, women make their own indispensable contributions to the economy of the society. The general myth is that it is the male who provides most of the food in the food-gathering–hunting society, but the truth is that some 80 percent of it is provided by the female. The men hunt, women do not, for they are far too occupied with their domestic duties; and furthermore, in many cultures they are actively discouraged from engaging in activities considered the exclusive prerogative of males—just as males are excluded from engaging in activities considered the exclusive preserve of females.

We see, then, that the division of labor between the sexes has its origin in the biologically determined different functions of male and female. This does not mean that the male is biologically more active or that he is biologically designed to be a hunter; it *does* mean that these roles are the *social consequences* of the biologically determined reproductive differences between the sexes. It is an error to assume that the female is by nature sedentary whereas the male is by nature active and mobile. Such activity differences do exist between male and female, but to a large extent they would seem to be secondary differences, *not* primary. Males have a metabolic rate that is between 5 and 6 percent higher than that of females, and from the earliest ages males are more active than females. Even the red blood cells are more numerous in the male, the red-cell count being, on the average, 4,800,000 in the male and 4,370,000 in the female. Since the red blood cells carry the oxygen on their surface membranes, it will be seen why the female requires fewer than the male: She doesn't require as much fuel.

The socially observed differences in activity between the sexes, it cannot be doubted, are to a large extent acquired rather than inherited. In short, these activity differences do not represent first nature, though they may become second nature. First nature is the biological equipment of potentialities with which one is born; second nature is what one's culture and society make of one, the habits one acquires.

Culture, the man-made part of the environment, is the way of life of a people, its institutions, customs, its pots and pans. The division of labor between the sexes represents a *cultural* expression of biological differences. The variety of cultural forms that this expression may take in different societies is enormous; what may be considered women's work in one may be deemed men's work in another. In some cultures men and women may engage in common activities that in other cultures are strictly separated along sexual lines. The important point to grasp is that the prescribed roles assigned to the sexes are not determined biologically but largely culturally. As Professor Ralph Linton has put it:

All societies prescribe different attitudes and activities to men and to women. Most of them try to rationalize these prescriptions in terms of the physiological differences between the sexes or their different roles in reproduction. However, a comparative study of the statuses ascribed to women and men in different cultures seems to show that while such factors may have served as a starting point for the development of a division the actual ascriptions are almost entirely determined by culture.[1]

[1] Ralph Linton, *The Study of Man* (New York: D. Appleton-Century Company, 1936), p. 116.

Roles and statuses serve to emphasize the character of social expectations and thus control the nature of the responses made to them.

The biological differences between the sexes obviously provide the grounds upon which are based the different social roles the sexes are expected to play. But the significance of the biological differences is often interpreted in such a manner as to convey the appearance of a natural connection between conditions that are, in fact, only artificially connected, that is, by misinterpretation. For example, in almost all cultures pregnancy, birth, and nursing are interpreted by both sexes as handicapping experiences; as a consequence women have been made to feel that by virtue of their biological functions they have been biologically, naturally, placed in an inferior position to men. But as we today well know, these biological functions of women are only minimally, if at all, handicapping.

It is worth paying some attention to the significance of the fact that in the fundamental role in which one would have thought it all too obviously clear that women were the superiors of men, namely, in their ability to bear and bring up children, women have been made to feel that their roles are handicapping ones. The evidence relating to the conditions of childbirth and child rearing in nonliterate societies is scant enough, but the indications are that, on the whole, women in nonliterate societies seem to have an easier time than they do in more complex ones. Unquestionably, under primitive conditions childbirth and child rearing are to some extent handicapping conditions *from the male viewpoint*. This is the conscious male viewpoint; the unconscious male viewpoint, there is much factual evidence to show, is of a very different nature. In almost all societies birth seems to have been culturally converted into a very much more complex, difficult, and handicapping process than it in fact is. In general it would seem that the more complex a society becomes, the more it tends to complicate the process of birth; one result of this is seen in the cultures of the Western world where women have been made to spend anything from ten days to three weeks in "confinement," as the reduction to helplessness so appropriately used to be called. With the advent of "natural childbirth," women are finding childbirth far from unpleasant and far from handicapping. Ambulatory surgery has influenced obstetrics to such an extent that the mother who has given birth is required to rise within two or three days of delivery of her child and within four or five days to return to her home! In some nonliterate societies some women take much less time than that to return to their normal household chores. In food-gathering–hunting cultures, such as those of the Bushman of South Africa and the Australian aborigines, the fact that a woman is pregnant or that an hour ago she gave birth to a child is generally responsible for little deviation from her customary manner of living, except for the additional task of nursing. It sometimes happens that on the march, in wandering from one food area to another, a woman falls out, gives birth to her child, catches up with her companions, and behaves very much as if nothing extraordinary had happened. If another child happens to be born to her a little too soon after the last one, it may be disposed of, for now it may constitute a real disability, since under the conditions of the food-gathering–hunting way of life it is difficult to take care of more than one infant at a time. There must be adequate spacing between children, not for this reason alone but also because the business of raising a child is considered to be virtually a full-time job and a matter not to be undertaken lightly.

Childbirth and nursing do introduce additional activities into the life of the female, but such activities do not necessarily constitute disadvantages. In comparison with certain forms of masculine mobility, and under certain social conditions, such activities *may* be disadvantages, and it would be wrong to underestimate them. It would, however, be equally wrong to overestimate such disadvantages; yet this has been done, and I believe the evidence strongly indicates that it has been deliberately, if to some extent unconsciously, done. If one can turn childbirth into a handicapping function, then that makes women so much more inferior to the sex that suffers from no such handicap. Persons who resort to such devices are usually concerned not so much with the inferiorities of others as with their own superiority. If one happens to be lacking in certain capacities with which the opposite sex is naturally endowed, and those capacities happen to be highly, if unacknowledgedly, valued, then one can compensate for one's own deficiency by devaluing the capacities of others. By turning capacities into handicaps, not only can one make their possessors feel inferior, but anyone lacking such capacities can then feel superior for very lack of them.

Ludicrous as the idea may appear to some, the fact is that men have been jealous of women's ability to give birth to children, and they have even envied their ability to menstruate; but men have not been content with turning these capacities into disabilities, for they have surrounded the one with handicapping rituals and the other with taboos that in most cases amount to punishments. They have even gone so far as to assert that pregnancy occurs in the male first, and that it is entirely dependent upon him whether the female becomes pregnant or not. For instance, among numerous Australian tribes it is the common belief that intercourse has no causative relation to pregnancy and that pregnancy is caused by the entry of a spirit child into the female.[2] In many of these tribes

[2] Ashley Montagu, *Coming into Being Among the Australian Aborigines*, 2nd ed. (London & Boston: Routledge, 1974).

it is the husband who first dreams that a spirit child has entered him. Should he desire a child, he tells his wife what has happened, and the spirit child is then transferred to her. Even then she is merely regarded as the incubator of the child planted in her by the male.

The idea is clearly expressed by Aeschylus (525–456 B.C.) in his *Eumenides* (628–31), in which Athene says, "The parent of that which is called her child is not really the *mother* of it, she is but the *nurse* of the newly conceived fetus. It is the male who is the author of its being, while she, as a stranger for a stranger [*i.e.*, no blood relation], preserves the young plant."

The very terms we use when we speak of male and female roles in reproduction, like the terms "male" and "female" themselves, and also "man" and "wo-man," make women subservient addenda to men and reflect the ignorance and prejudice that have characterized the dominant male attitudes regarding the female. The male "fertilizes," "fecundates," or "impregnates" the female. The truth, however, is quite otherwise. The process of reproduction is not one-sided; its antecedent condition is the fusion of two cells, the female ovum and the male sperm. It is not that an ovum is rendered fertile by the sperm but that ovum and sperm *together* contribute to the initiation of those further processes that result in the development of the conceptus. The ovum has a volume approximately eighty-five thousand times greater than that of the sperm, presumably because it carries the nutriment necessary for the development of the early conceptus.

Menstruation has been regarded among many peoples as woman's method of getting rid of the evil humors that were believed to accumulate in the body. Since men lack such a natural means of achieving this desired end, the Australian aborigines perform an operation on the adolescent youth, at his second initiation, which is called "subincision." This operation consists of slitting open the urinary tube (the urethra) on the underside of the penis from the scrotum to the external orifice. A stone is then inserted into the subincised penis to keep the urethra permanently open. Such a subincised penis is called by the same name as that of the female vulva. There can be not the least doubt that among other things the purpose of this operation represents an attempt to imitate the female external genitals. Every so often, especially at ceremonies and initiations, the subincised penis will be incised to make it bleed in imitation of the female's menstruation. Precisely similar operations are performed by the natives of the island of Wogeo, one of the Schouten Islands of the north coast of Netherlands New Guinea. Periodic incision of the penis and the flow of blood thus induced is often referred to as men's menstruation; such men are subject to much the same prohibitions as menstruating women, but the flow of blood is considered to be a necessary cleansing process.[3]

What the female possesses by natural endowment the male must, at great pain and suffering to himself, periodically produce by art; this constitutes a further ground of jealousy of, and resentment against, the female. A similar operation is therefore performed upon girls at puberty. During this operation the clitoris and both labia are cut away, at which time, in some Australian groups, all the initiated men proceed to have intercourse with the girl. Such an operation is performed in the thousands at the present time in the territories of Egypt and far up along both sides of the Nile. Furthermore, in the North African regions where this operation is performed the vulva is sewn up in such a manner as to leave only a small orifice for the exudation of the menstrual and urinary fluids; this operation is known as "infibula-

[3] Ashley Montagu, "The Origin of Subincision in Australia," *Oceania*, VIII (1937), 193–207.

tion." Here the jealousy of the male has gone so far as to limit virtually completely the female's capacity for pregnancy and childbirth. When the girl reaches marriageable age, the orifice may be enlarged to admit her husband's penis, and it will be opened up, by incision, shortly before childbirth, and after childbirth sewn up again! [4]

Should anyone be inclined to think that it is only non-literate peoples and benighted heathen who indulge in such sadistic practices at the expense of the female, it has only to be pointed out that not so many years ago some American surgeons were performing clitoridectomies by the dozen, while today surgeons are yearly sedulously castrating thousands of women, for even though the ovaries are not removed that is what the operation of hysterectomy really is. How many of these operations are really necessary? Can it be that in some cases the unconscious motivations for such operations differ from those consciously alleged?

Man's jealousy of woman's capacity to bear children is nowhere better exhibited than in the Old Testament creation story in which man is caused to give birth (from one of his ribs) to woman:

And the rib, which the Lord God had taken from man, made he a woman, and brought her unto the man.

And Adam said, This is now bone of my bones, and flesh of my flesh: she shall be called Woman, because she was taken out of Man (*Genesis*, 2).

A frequent subject of medieval art is the delivery of Eve from Adam's side. God, it has been remarked, may have created man first, but that may be because he was

---

[4] For a full account of infibulation, see H. H. Ploss, M. and P. Bartels, *Woman*, I (St. Louis, Mo.: V. Mosby Company, 1935), 353–363. See also Ashley Montagu, "Infibulation and Defibulation in the Old and New Worlds," *American Anthropologist*, XLVII (1945), 464–467.

merely practicing before creating the finished article, woman.

Milton considered the creation of woman a mistake. In *Paradise Lost* he wrote:

> *O why did god*
> *Creator wise, that peopl'd highest Heav'n*
> *With Spirits Masculine, create at last*
> *This noveltie on Earth, this fair defect*
> *Of Nature, and not fill the World at once*
> *With Men as Angels without Feminine,*
> *Or find some other way to generate*
> *Mankind?*

Possibly the answer lies in Dr. Samuel Johnson's reply to a lady who asked him to define the difference between man and woman: "I can't conceive, Madam," he replied. "Can you?"

We begin to see, then, how it may have come about that childbirth as well as menstruation were converted from perfectly healthy natural phenomena into a handicap and a "curse." Men project their unconscious wishes upon the screen of their society and make their institutions and their gods in the image of their desires. Their envy of woman's physiological powers causes them to feel weak and inferior, and fear is often added to jealousy. An effective way for men to protect themselves against women, as well as to punish them, is to depreciate their capacities by depreciating their status. One can deny the virtues of women's advantages by treating them as disadvantages and by investing them with mysterious or dangerous properties. By making women objects of fear and something to be avoided as unclean, one can lower the cultural status of women by simple inversion. Their biological advantages are demoted to the status of cultural disadvantages, and as cultural disadvantages they are then converted into biological disadvantages. Once this is achieved, there need be no end to the belief in the cultural and biological disadvantages of these traits.

It is not here being suggested that this sort of thinking occurs, except occasionally, on the conscious level; the suggestion is that it does occur on the unconscious level, a suggestion for which there is a very great deal of evidence, mainly of an anthropological and psychoanalytic nature, of the kind that has already been mentioned.[5]

From an early age females are conditioned to believe that menstruation is a curse and a handicap. Pregnancy, they have been taught, puts them in a precarious condition, while childbirth has been enveloped with so many myths and mysteries and dangers that most women in the Western world have until recently rarely approached or experienced the event without foreboding and anxiety —and this holds true for the sympathetic husband, too.

We have fallen heir, through our social heredity and our traditions, to a set of beliefs concerning the "biological disadvantages" of females. We have already seen what some of the origins of these beliefs may have been, and why, in part, they still continue to be maintained. These beliefs are almost wholly unsound. We know today that menstruation is neither mysterious nor malignant but a perfectly healthy, normal function of women.[6] Pregnancy need be neither precarious nor handicapping, nor need childbirth or childbearing. If women have been

---

5 Edith Jacobson, "The Development of the Wish for a Child in Boys," *The Psychoanalytic Study of the Child*, V (New York: International Universities Press, 1950), 139–152; Bruno Bettelheim, *Symbolic Wounds* (New York: Free Press, 1954); Leon Salzman, "Psychology of the Female," *Archives of General Psychiatry*, XVII (1967), 195–203.

6 Ashley Montagu, "Physiology and the Origins of the Menstrual Prohibitions," *Quarterly Review of Biology*, XV (1940), 211–20; W. N. Stephens, "A Cross-Cultural Study of Menstrual Taboos," *Genetic Psychology Monographs*, LXIV (1961), 385.

led to believe that these functions are handicapping, and that women must therefore play second fiddle to the male of the species, both women and men perhaps may now better understand how this belief came into being, and perhaps endeavor to make the functions of women something closer to the achievement of the great privileges they are. But this is a theme we shall take up in a later and more appropriate place. For the present let us return to a consideration of the manner in which certain of the other alleged disabilities of women came into being.

Owing to the enlarging experiences that fall to the male in consequence of his roles as the hunter and maker of implements, he develops certain highly valued traits and skills. These are a broad experience and varied knowledge of an environment larger than that which the female experiences, the increase in knowledge which such experience brings, and the ability to make things that the female is not called upon to make, especially hunting implements. It will readily be seen that such traits immediately give their possessor an advantage over their nonpossessor. It will also be readily understood why it is that men, under such conditions, consider women their inferiors and themselves incomparably more important, for while it is woman's work to concern herself with the preservation of the individual, men are concerned with no less than the perpetuation of the race. Were it not for the basic support that men provide for the family (so they consider), the race would die out. Even though this is, and always has been, a highly questionable proposition, such, nevertheless, has always been the opinion of the "head of the family." It is an open question whether the real holder-together and support of the family in the psychological, if not entirely in the material sense, has not always been the wife and mother. However that may be, he who pays the piper calls the tune, and the head of the family has always demanded the respect due to a superior person, and it has been given him—but always at the cost of making all other members of his family feel inferior. And, indeed, by comparison everyone else in the family *was* inferior, for the wife possessed no such skills as her husband, nor was she anywhere nearly as knowledgeable about so many of the things her husband had experienced; furthermore, he was bigger and stronger than she. The children, of course, were even more inferior to their father than was their mother, and they would naturally grow up having no doubt of the mother's inferiority to their father.

Thus everyone, including Mother, would be convinced that Father was a superior person and that Mother was at best a mere second-rater. Everyone drew the erroneous conclusion from the cultural facts that these differences of superiority and inferiority were biologically determined; women, it was assumed, were naturally inferior to men, and that was that. And, in reality, to the present day, women have remained inferior to men practically everywhere in the world for much the same reasons that they were, from the earliest times, first discovered to be inferior: *They were practically never given equal opportunities with men to develop their capacities; the opportunities for the development of their intelligence and tribal skills were severely restricted by what was traditionally considered permissible to women; they were prejudged rather than fairly judged; and they were condemned to a servitude from which they could never emerge unless granted the opportunity to do so.*

In the 1840's a writer in *Godey's Lady's Book* put it very plainly: "As a general hint there was much wisdom in the advice given by an old mother to a young one: Stimulate the sensibilities of your boys and blunt those of your girls." Depressing advice, but well adapted to the realities of the time. Charlotte Brontë's friend Mary Taylor wrote, in 1845, "There are no means for a woman to live in England, but by teaching, sewing or washing. The last is the best. The best paid, the least unhealthy, and the most free."

In 1864 Walter Bagehot, the famous English economist, wrote to Emily Davies, the woman's rights leader, "I assure you I am not an 'enemy of women.' I am very favourable to their employment as *labourers* or in any other *menial* capacity. I have, however, doubts as to the likelihood of their succeeding in business as capitalists. I am sure the nerves of most women would break down under the anxiety and that most of them are utterly destitute of the disciplined reticence and self-constraint necessary to every sort of cooperation.

"Two thousand years hence you may have changed it all, but the *present* woman will only flirt with men and quarrel with one another."

The truth is that until 1914 women lived in a world in which they were forced to be totally dependent on men, and were deprived of all legal autonomy as human beings.

Feelings of weakness and inferiority have their roots in other than purely cultural factors. It is a matter of fact that men are usually bigger and more powerful than women. Being bigger and more obviously powerful generally makes the bigger and more powerful person feel and act in a "big" and powerful manner. In the presence of such persons the smaller and the less powerful are likely to feel "dwarfed." At any rate, where the sexes are concerned, the factors of size and power, added to other prerogatives and statuses, put the male decidedly in the position of dominance. Women have been so long conditioned in the environment of masculine dominance that they have come to expect the male to be dominant and the female subservient. The psychologic subservience of the female has assumed innumerable ramifications in almost all human societies and constitutes yet another illustration of the effects of the cultural differentiation of the sexes.

Among the many ways in which the downgrading of women traditionally proceeds, one of the foremost is through the formal processes of "education." In a study of children's textbooks and personality development Drs. I. L. Child, E. H. Potter, and E. M. Levine found that the third-grade-level readers they examined presented females in an unfavorable and indifferent light. Females were nurturing and gentle but seldom active, adventurous, constructive, achieving, or worthy of recognition. "Girls and women are thus being shown as sociable, kind and timid, but inactive, unambitious and uncreative." The characters in the stories who were nurtured and given support were generally female, "suggesting that females are in a relatively helpless position." On the other hand, the knowledgeable people were males. "Males, in short, are being portrayed as the bearers of knowledge and wisdom." In some instances females were portrayed as being morally inferior to the male. They were portrayed as acquiring things in socially disapproved ways much more often than males, and less often by the socially approved means of effort and work. They were shown as lazy twice as often as males. In addition to their being slighted in these ways by comparison with males, males were predominantly the heroes of the stories, 73 percent being males and only 27 percent females. "The implication," write the authors of this study, "of this difference for a girl is that being female is a pretty bad thing, that the only people even in everyday life who are worth writing about or reading about are boys and men. If the content of these readers is typical of other social influences, small wonder that girls might develop for this reason alone an inferiority complex about their sex. . . . The many schoolgirls

who will at some future time have to make their own
living are failing, if they identify with female characters,
to receive the same training in the development of motives for work and achievement that boys are receiving.
To the extent that this distinction is characteristic of
many other aspects of the training the child receives
from his environment, it should cause little wonder that
women are sometimes less fitted for creative work and
achievement than men of similar aptitude, for there is
certainly much difference in the motivational training
they receive for it." [7]

It is the general rule throughout the animal kingdom
that wherever one sex is larger or physically more powerful than the other, the larger or physically more
powerful sex will occupy the position of dominance.
Man, we know, is something more than an animal, but
not all men have quite realized that fact. If, as Plato
said, civilization is the victory of persuasion over force,
it may be that men may yet be persuaded to consider
some of the origins of their sexual dominance, and even
to learn that the force of argument is eventually stronger
and more beneficial in its effects than the argument of
force.

It has already been pointed out that there is a remarkable parallel between the phenomena of race prejudice and the prejudice against women. This is nicely
illustrated by an editorial comment on a woman's suffrage meeting held in Syracuse, New York. The editorial
appeared in the New York *Herald*, in the issue of 12
September 1852, and was probably written by the elder
Bennett. Among other things, the editorial said:

How did woman first become subject to man, as she now is
all over the world? By her nature, her sex, just as the negro

[7] I. L. Child, E. H. Potter, and E. M. Levine, "Children's Textbooks
and Personality Development," *Psychological Monographs*, LX (1946),
1–7, 45–53.

is and always will be to the end of time, inferior to the white race and, therefore, doomed to subjection; but she is happier than she would be in any other condition, just because it is the law of her nature. . . .

How often do men mistake their prejudices for the laws of nature!

Everything that has been said about almost any alleged "inferior race" has been said by men about women. We have already heard that their brains are smaller, that their intelligence is lower, that they are not very good at arithmetic, that one can't trust them to govern their own affairs, that they are like children, emotional, unoriginal, uncreative, unintellectual, with a severely limited attention span, and so on, through the whole dreary calendar. These are the familiar arguments of the racists, their stock in trade; and every one of them has been urged as a fact against the Black as well as against women in general. I hope that no reader of this book is naïve enough to imagine that proof of the erroneousness of these beliefs would be sufficient to eliminate either race prejudice or the prejudice against women; for just as the race problem is not really a race problem at all but a problem in human relations, so the prejudice against women is not a simple matter of antifeminism or whatnot but also a problem in human relations. Until we solve the human-relations problem, we shall solve neither these nor any other difficulties of human beings. It is part of the purpose of this book to show how this problem may be solved. Man is himself a problem in search of a solution, and his prejudices against minority groups—and women constitute a social minority group if not a numerical one—are groping expressions of his confused attempts to solve his problem.

When men understand that the best way to solve their own problem is to help women solve those that men have created for women, they will have taken one of the first significant steps toward its solution. And what is woman's greatest problem? Man. For man has created and maintained her principal difficulties, and until man solves his own difficulties there can be no wholly satisfactory solution of woman's. Once again it is like the Black's problem, which is the white man. Until the white man solves his personal difficulties, the Black will continue to afford a convenient scapegoat. These difficulties in human relations are not simply problems in the communication of facts. You don't cure a person suffering from delusions by telling him that he is playing tricks with reality and that the facts are other than he asserts them to be. Deep and complex psychological conditions are involved; we must make the patient aware of them before we can hope for any possibility of a cure. Prevention is so much better than cure, so painless, and so much less costly in the service of the good health of our society, that it is worth hanging a big question mark on some of the things we take most for granted.

3.

Biological Facts and Social Consequences

IN ALL SOCIETIES women have played a much more important role than their menfolk have been generally inclined to admit. After all, if one is afflicted with feelings of inferiority—as the male is with respect to the female—a strong overcompensatory tendency to play cock o' the roost is likely to develop. It is difficult to admit, even though the dark suspicion may have dawned on one, that women are one's equals, and—perish the thought—they certainly are not one's superiors. After all, is not the evidence, the biological evidence, of male superiority unequivocally clear?

The answer is that it is far from clear that man is biologically superior to woman, and that, on the contrary—as we shall see—the evidence indicates that woman is, on the whole, biologically superior to man. Since we have already used the term "superior" without having defined it, and since it is a significant term for our discussion, we had better define it now. The term is used in its common sense as meaning being of better quality or of higher nature or character.

Of better quality or of higher nature or character in

respect to what? The question is a crucial one, and upon its correct answer turns the whole theme of this book. The soundness of the book's argument depends upon the soundness of the answer returned to the question. That answer is: Superiority in any trait, whether bio-logical or social, is measured by the extent to which that trait confers survival benefits upon the person and the group. If you function in such a way as to live longer, be more resistant, healthier, and behave in a manner generally calculated to enable you and your progeny to survive more efficiently than others who do not function as efficiently, then by the measure of our definition of superiority you are superior to the others. The reference here is not simply to immediate survival but to the long-term survival of the group. And by group, for the purposes of this discussion, I mean the immediate family, and then the social group of which the family is a part, and finally the whole group of mankind—humanity.

Allowing for the usual variability, man, for example, is bigger and physically more powerful than woman. Are these, then, traits in which man is superior to woman? In other words, do greater size and muscular power make for greater survival? The comparison is between men and women and *not* between men and other men. There can be no doubt that culturally we value tall men and powerful ones, but we may legiti-mately entertain the suspicion that this, too, is a male-determined value. In fact, we place a negative value upon unusually tall as well as upon powerful women. Women almost always prefer a man who is taller than themselves. Why? Can it be that women have been taught to "look up" to men so that (to give the unex-pressed corollary) men may "look down" upon them? May not the bruited advantages of larger size and muscular power constitute yet another of the male-made myths foisted upon an unsuspecting feminine world?

Are larger size and greater muscular power biological advantages? The dinosaurs had a long run for their money, but eventually size and muscular power proved their undoing, and the monstrous creatures vanished from the face of the earth. Man, by means of the development of size and power, finds himself in a dangerous position, in a deadly parallel with the long-extinct dinosaurs. My reference is not simply to the misuse of size and power; it is intended to suggest that the very existence of size and power seems to constitute in itself an incentive and an irritant to man to use them.

With the accumulation of armaments there is a strong tendency not to control them but to employ them. In terms of size and muscular power man has exercised a physical *and* psychological supremacy over woman. However, that is a very different thing from saying that from the sociobiological point of view such supremacy endows man with a superiority over woman. If, as a consequence of the possession of greater size and muscular power, one is better able to pull and move heavy loads, run faster, and better accomplish all those things that minister to the survival of the person and the group, then it should be plain that men are in these respects superior to women. But while men have, in part, used their size and greater muscular power in a manner calculated to confer survival benefits upon themselves and upon the group, they have also misused these qualities in such a manner as to confer negative survival benefits upon themselves and upon the group. The muscle man likes to feel his bumps and is, therefore, inclined to be bumptious. His size inclines him to throw his weight around, and not only to persuade his woman that he loves her most when he is "showing her who's boss" and "treating her rough," but also to show his fellows in the pecking order that he is not to be trifled with. Since there are likely to be other men around who feel much the same way, trouble is inevitable. Such conflicts as arise within the group in this way make no contribution to its better survival. Many a good and valuable man has been unnecessarily lost to the group by asserting his muscles rather than by using his mind, and the group has suffered as a consequence. Vendettas and internecine conflicts are essentially masculine activities, and the most pathological form that such activities take, namely, war, is exclusively a masculine invention and ghastliness. Such activities do not contribute to the survival of the individual or of the group.

Since greater size and physical power are overt evidences of masculinity, boys are in most cultures encouraged to demonstrate their "superior" masculinity by indulging in games, sports, and other activities that are at the same time calculated to underscore the inferiority in power of the girls. And this is done at a time when the girls may be, at the same chronologic ages, larger in size and physically more powerful than the boys! Boys are encouraged to be tough and rough, to play with guns and other weapons of destruction, and to go in for sports that are "rugged." In addition, because boys are supposed to be able to endure more than girls, boys may be corporeally punished (and so unconsciously encouraged in the development of additional hostilities), whereas girls are usually punished by deprivation or by the assignment of unpleasant chores.

It should be clear, then, that the greater size and power of the male may constitute biological advantages or sociobiological disadvantages, depending upon the manner in which they are used. In a society in which the strong destroy themselves, it is obviously an advantage not to be strong.

Here we are concerned with the relation of the male's greater size and physical power to the comparatively lesser size and physical power of the female. It is clear that man has used his physical advantages to maintain woman in a subservient position, and in human societies has established a physical and social supremacy over the female. Because the muscles account for 42 percent of the total body weight in the male and only 36 percent in the female, the male is able to implement his commands and to enforce his will by the adequate exercise of his muscular powers. Obedience is commanded in this way when it can be in no other. The long training of men in securing obedience through the use of force is almost certainly related to the ease with which men fall back upon this means of compelling attention and securing obedience.

As the distinguished zoologist lately of McGill University has said, "Men and boys are troublesome creatures, but being larger, stronger and louder than the females they have succeeded in putting over the biggest bluff the earth has ever seen." And perhaps not altogether with tongue in cheek Professor Berrill adds, "For when you come to the point, what use are males apart from keeping some sweet young things happy and keeping other males at bay?" [1]

I am not writing an indictment of man. I am writing part of the story of man trying to be human. Men have been confused and scared for a long time, and like most scared and confused creatures conscious of their physical superiority to the opposite sex or to members of their own sex they are likely to take on something of the

[1] N. J. Berrill, "Women Should Run the World," *Maclean's Magazine,* 15 (February 1958), 8.

character of the bully. Men have browbeaten women from time immemorial, and one of the subtlest of the ways in which they have done so is through the development of elaborate codes of chivalry and etiquette. The forms of chivalry and etiquette, though they may have been and may continue to be much valued by women, were originally not really intended as friendly acts; they represented the behavior of a patronizing superior who, in effect, was saying: "As your superior, I am called upon to give you my support, and make things easier for you. You, as an inferior person, are in all respects less capable than I; and as long as you continue to recognize these facts, and remain submissive and dependent, I will continue to be polite to you." Chivalry was thus a kind of fictitious benevolence, the gloss put by good manners on selfishness, self-conceit, and contempt for the rights of women. . . . In other words a putdown.

Observe how chivalry and the ordinary rules of politeness break down as soon as women begin to compete with men on their own home grounds. Men no longer offer their seats to women in conveyances. "Don't get up," I have heard men say, "they're just as strong as we are." In short, when one could keep women in their "proper place," chivalry was a useful device, but when women begin to assert themselves as equals chivalry is no longer esteemed to serve a useful purpose. This is not to deny, however, that the chivalry of many men has been a genuine unconscious or conscious recognition of the value and quality of women, and of their debt to them.

Because, by virtue of his greater physical power, man has been able to determine the fate and development of woman, men and women have come to assume that it was natural for men to do so, and both have come to mistake their prejudices for the laws of nature. That men may bully women into a position of subservience is not a biological fact but a cultural one, a cultural misuse of a biological condition. This is a very different thing from saying that women are biologically determined to occupy a subservient relation to the male and that the male is biologically determined to keep the female in such a subservient position. Female subservience is a culturally, *not* a biologically, produced condition. It is one of the consequences of the misuse of masculine power.

As Thomas Jefferson wrote, "The stronger sex imposes on the weaker. It is civilization alone which replaces women in their enjoyment of their natural equality." [2]

At this juncture it may be useful to list some of the presumed social consequences of the biological differences between the sexes, thereby enabling us to perceive at a glance some of the biological pegs upon which men have hung the cultural disabilities of women.

Looking at Table 1, we see that there are quite a number of biological sex differences and their social consequences which we have not yet considered.

The larger size and higher metabolism of the male finds functional expression in his greater need for food than the female, and in a greater expenditure of energy. One of the presumed social consequences of these differences is the male's greater drive in work and in achievement. As we have already noted earlier, it is extremely doubtful whether the physiological differences in metabolism and their functional expression have any real connection with the male's alleged greater drive in work and achievement.

I am not the first to suggest, and I am sure I shall

[2] Thomas Jefferson, *Notes on the State of Virginia 1781–1785*, Paris, 1785 (in Saul Padover, *The Complete Jefferson*, New York: Tudor Publishing Co., 1943, p. 607).

Table I. Some Presumed Social Consequences of the Biological Differences Between the Sexes *

BIOLOGICAL SEX DIFFERENCES	FUNCTIONAL EXPRESSION	SOCIAL CONSEQUENCES
Men bigger, more powerful	Greater capacity for heavy labor	Dominance of males. Different jobs, roles, assigned each sex; in anticipation different training given to each
Women bear children, nurse them	Movements impeded, kept closer to home	
Greater muscular development in male	Urge to physical exertion, greater pride in it	Greater interest of male in sports, etc.
Male's larger size, higher metabolism, greater activity	Need for more food, more expenditure of energy	Greater drive in work, achievement
Lesser strength of female	Inability to cope with male physically	"Feminine" devices to achieve ends
Male conscious of strength	Tendency of men to treat women gently	Codes of chivalry, etiquette
Differences in genitalia and body	Garments adjusted differently for comfort, utility	Differences in dress, styles
Earlier puberty in girls	Ready for mating earlier	Girls permitted to marry; reach "age of consent" earlier

* Based on a table in Amram Scheinfeld's *Women and Men* (New York: Harcourt, Brace & Company, 1944).

Table I (*continued*)

BIOLOGICAL SEX DIFFERENCES	FUNCTIONAL EXPRESSION	SOCIAL CONSEQUENCES
Menstruation	Effects on body, mind; consciousness of blood issue, other symptoms	Taboos on women, psychological and social restraint
Role in sex relationships	Women can have intercourse without desire; men cannot	Prostitution confined largely to women, rape to men
Pregnancy in women	Greater risk in sexual relationships, uncertainty of paternity	"Double standard" of conduct, stricter codes of behavior for unmarried girls and women
Menopause in women	Reproductive capacity ends much earlier than men's	Men's marriage chances continue beyond women's
Female biologically more resistant to disease, bodily upsets	Her life span longer; surplus of women increasing	Threat to monogamous marriage system; problems of spinsterhood and widowhood

not be the last, that the male's drive in work and achievement may actually be the consequence of his recognition of his biological inferiority with respect to the female's creative capacity to conceive and create human beings. One of the ways in which the male may compensate for this biological inferiority is by work and by achievement. By keeping the means of making a livelihood almost exclusively a masculine prerogative, men have unconsciously, as well as consciously, been able to satisfy themselves that they are by nature the "breadwinners," the pillars of society, and the guarantors of the race. Hence, the great opposition to women when they begin to enter into "competition" with men in earning a living. Married men, in particular, frequently object to their wives' working; they consider it, somehow, a reflection upon themselves. They fear it will be said that they are unable to support their family. "My wife doesn't have to work. Why should she?" The arguments will be familiar to the reader, whether married or not.

Let men honestly ask themselves why they object to women working, particularly their wives, even though they may be largely free of those domestic duties that would otherwise keep them at home. Some quite illuminating answers might begin to break through the barrier of the unconscious. A wife, or almost any woman, working for a living, particularly in a field considered the special preserve of the male, is held by many males to constitute a challenge to their masculinity. When the question comes up of the employment of a woman in some position that has hitherto been filled by a male, masculine reactions are often very revealing. The violence of the emotion and the irrational behavior that many males have exhibited, and many still continue to exhibit on such occasions, indicate how profoundly they are disturbed by the idea of women working outside the home.

The male, in all societies, is at greater risk than the female. As Ritchie has pointed out, "The female, as she grows older and develops, has before her in more or less continuous relationship, the model of her mother.

The man, as he grows through life, begins his life also in primary relationship to a maternal object but he has to give it up, he has to leave off identification with the mother, he has to take on the full male role. Males have to switch identification during development, and all sorts of things can go wrong in this." And, unfortunately, they frequently do. The male has a much more difficult time than the female in growing up and separating himself from the loving mother and in identifying himself with a father with whom he is nowhere nearly as deeply involved as he remains with the mother. This often puts a strain upon him. The switch in identification he is called upon to make results in something of a conflict. This he usually seeks to resolve by, in part, rejecting the mother and relegating her to a status inferior to that into which he has, so to speak, been thrust. Masculine antifeminism can be regarded as a reaction-formation designed to oppose the strong unconscious trend towards mother-worship. When the male's defenses are down, when he is *in extremis*, when he is dying, his last, like his first, word, is likely to be "mother," in a resurgence of his feeling for the mother he has never really repudiated, but from whom, at the overt level, he has been forced to disengage himself.

Marriage, that "ghastly public confession of a strictly private intention," as some Victorian once put it, used to be the one institution by means of which the female could be securely kept in her place. Men used to be able to work and to create without feeling challenged by their own wives. Wives used to stay at home, have babies, and look after them and the "breadwinner" too. God was in his Heaven and all was right with the world.

As another Victorian male put it, "A man whose life is of any value should think of his wife as a nurse."

Most of the 33,000,000 women in the labor force in the United States in 1973 have demonstrated that they can work as hard as men at almost all occupations and that they do a great deal better at some than men ever did—clerical work, for example, and work demanding great precision and delicacy of touch. Men, therefore, cannot honestly object to women on the ground of lack of capacity or inefficiency. Men have resisted the "intrusion" of women into their workaday world to the last ditch, and many are still doing it. Why? May it not be that such men feel that the working woman constitutes a threat to their belief in themselves as the pillars of society? to the foundations upon which society rests, the "creators" of civilization? May it not be that men don't want their fears and insecurities about women disturbed? In the unconscious these fears and insecurities are buried so deep beneath the surface of an ocean of repressions and rationalizations that no shoal or rock is likely to be encountered. Nevertheless, all one has to do to rock the boat is to introduce a woman in a capacity in which men have always served. The best way, therefore, to avoid such disturbances is to restrict women to the role of the helpless female who wouldn't know what to do with an oar or an engine if her life depended upon it. It's "*Man* the boats. Women and children first." And, of course, a certain number of men have to get into the boats; otherwise, the women wouldn't be able to manage.

The origin of the English word "woman" indicates that the female's very right to social existence was determined in the light of her secondary relationship to the male, for the word was originally "wifman," that is, "wife-man," the wife of the man; in the fourteenth century the *f* was dropped and the word became "wiman," and later on "woman." Men unconsciously have desired to keep women in a secondary position, and all the rationalizations they have offered for keeping her there have avoided the statement of their actual motivation, because in most cases they have not consciously been aware of the nature of that motivation. Men must work and women must spin, because if women stop spinning and start working, man's claim to "creativity" and indispensability as breadwinner is undermined—and this he must resist.

Such motivations seem to be even clearer with respect to achievement or creativity proper. If men cannot conceive, become pregnant, and bear a child, they can conceive great ideas and great works, gestate them, and be delivered of them in the form of all the things that make up our complex civilization: art, science, philosophy, music, machinery, bridges, dams, automobiles, kitchen gadgetry, and the million and one things men create and women buy. How often have we heard men exclaim, "That's my baby," when they have been referring to some product of their creation, whether it be an idea or an object? True enough, it is a way of speaking and may represent merely an analogical expression. Perhaps, and perhaps not. "These are the children of my brain," is another such expression. "I want to nurse this idea," is yet another. And there are many more. Why, it may be asked, should men use such expressions when in practically every other instance they use purely masculine phraseology and take great pains to avoid anything suggestive of the feminine? To be "pregnant with ideas," to be "delivered of a great idea," to "give birth to a plan"—may not these and other obstetrical expressions possibly indicate, when used by males, an unconscious desire to imitate the biological creativity of the female? The conversion process takes the form: "Well, if I can't create and give birth to biological babies, I can, at least, create and give birth to their social equivalents." Man's drive to achievement can, at least in part, be interpreted as an unconsciously motivated attempt to compensate for the lack of biological creativity. Witness how men have used their creativeness in the arts, sciences, and technologies as proof of their own superiority and the inferiority of women!

The fact is that men have had far greater opportunities for this kind of cultural creativity than women, and in this respect they have had a far more profoundly motivated drive to achieve than women. The evidence strongly suggests that were women motivated by as strong drives to achieve as men, and afforded equal opportunities to do so, they would at least be every bit as successful as men. Because women are for some time yet likely to remain, on the whole, less strongly motivated than men, I think it probable that men will continue to show a higher frequency of achievement, *not* because they are naturally superior but because their opportunities will remain greater, and because, among other things, they are overcompensating for a natural incapacity—the incapacity to bear babies.

The female's inability to cope with the physically stronger male obliges her, from an early age, to develop traits that will enable her to secure her ends by other means. Being forced to sharpen her wits upon the whetstone of the male's obduracy, the female develops a sharper intelligence. From their earliest years girls find it necessary to pay attention to nuances and small signs of which the crass male rarely recognizes the existence. Such small signs and signals tell the girl what she wants to know, and she is usually ready with her plan for action before the male has begun to act. I am not suggesting that women naturally have better brains than men. Perhaps they have. I don't know. But in picking up the nuances in life, the different shades of meaning; in seeing and getting to the point quickly, let men ask themselves the question, and frankly answer it: Which is the superior sex? Let it be remembered that I am not speaking about all women any more than I am speaking about all men; I am speaking about women and men in general. There are slow-witted members of both sexes just as there are quick-witted ones. My point is that women are on the whole more quick-witted than men, not because they are born that way (though a firm case that they are could be made on the basis of natural and social selection over a long period of time), but because culturally they have been forced to develop a sharpness of attention to small detail of which the less sensitive male remains quite unaware. Thus woman's intuition is something more than merely man's transparency—constituting a comment, possibly, on man's comparative opacity.

Woman's training in picking up such subliminal signs, which hardly every impinge upon the consciousness of the male, is in part responsible for her greater thoughtfulness, tact, and discretion; there are, however, many other factors that contribute to form these qualities in women. When one has a stubborn mule in the house, one has to learn to get around him. Women early developed a strategy of devices or "artful dodges" for dealing with the problem. Swooning, weeping, hysteria, the vapors, and other emotional simulations of "feminine weakness" were, up to the beginning of the twentieth century, standard equipment. The utterly dependent, clinging-vine pose is, of course, still with us. With some, it is to be feared, the "little-woman" attitude is anything but a pose. Such females tend to be so infantile that they have a powerful need to feel dependent upon a "strong" person—usually, but not necessarily always, a male. And, of course, a large number of females are brought up to believe that their natural state is to be dependent upon a male; in fact, many of them are taught to avoid all evidence in themselves of independence and to cultivate those traits that will appeal to the protective "instincts" of the male. Such females may acquire so high a competence in the use of "feminine tricks" that they themselves may come to believe them to be natural. In many women these devices have become almost second nature, and it is very difficult to distinguish between what is primary and what is secondary or acquired in human nature.

How strong the desire to be a clinging vine is in some women was forcibly brought home to me in the case of a student of mine, a very attractive young woman of about twenty-five who had already been married and divorced twice. She wished to marry again; she could see no purpose to her life except marriage. I suggested to her that she had a good mind and ought to do something useful with it. Her answer, literally, was: "I'm the clinging-vine type. I couldn't be any good at studies." Striking a bargain with her, I sent her to study with a brilliant colleague at a neighboring university. The essence of our agreement was that if she could prove to herself that she really had brains, she was to continue her studies, take her degree, and possibly think of making a profession of the subject in which she said she had some interest. At the end of the year she was at the head of a class of sixty students! My colleague took special pains to discuss her abilities with me and thanked me for sending him such a bright student. The sequel to the story is that as soon as the results of her examinations were announced, she immediately disappeared, and neither my colleague nor I saw her again until many years afterward. The shock of discovering that she really had brains and that she could, if she wanted to, rely upon her own merits for a living was more than she could bear; it was a fact that she refused to face, for its consequences were unpleasant to her even in contemplation. She married a third time, and I lost touch with her. I hope she finally came to rest.

The varieties of techniques women have been forced

to develop in order to cope with the male have had many unfortunate consequences—for both sexes. Under the circumstances this was a thoroughly unavoidable development. Women have to keep their eye on the main chance; they have to be constantly on their guard, with their antennae always extended, and all this without appearing to do so, unobtrusively operating on the appropriate wavelength and picking up the proper signals without anyone noticing, as it were. All this makes for a certain artificiality. Elegantly decorated, such artificiality is not displeasing to men, even when they are able to distinguish it as such, any more than the artificially deformed feet of Chinese women were displeasing to the perpetrators of such deformities, for it was considered beautiful to have feet that peeped like mice from beneath the skirts or trousers of women. The artificialities of the women of Western civilization possess an elegance of a different kind, for they represent a contrived confession of inferiority on the part of the female. It is a form of feminine wooing of the male. There he sits, this godlike creature, upon his throne, and all women who come before him must genuflect before him—and they do, or at least most of them do. Men, of course, do everything in their power to constrain women to maintain these artificial, disingenuous attitudes.

The most effective feminine devices to which women resort in dealing with the male are sexual. This is a province that women have made their own. Even Sigmund Freud, that genius in the study of human nature, was badly deceived upon this point, for he mistook the great *cultural* emphasis placed by our species on sex as a biologically motivated function. On the contrary, our emphasis on sex is one of the unfortunate social consequences of the inferior position in which women have been placed by men. Under such conditions sex becomes one of the principal means by which they can both protect and advance themselves and secure their ends. Sex is, of course, a biological drive; but what is not a biological drive, but a cultural mushrooming of a means by which the female may find her way about in the world, is the social expression of sex. This mushrooming has been forced by the male. As a consequence, sex has been given an emphasis and value that magnify out of all proportion its real place and importance in the organic scheme of human needs. Socially, sex has become almost a pathologic growth. Its beauty and true meaning have largely become perverted and deformed to degrading ends and purposes. The true significance of love and sex has become beclouded to such an extent that few people in our culture really understand what it is. Sex is equated with intercourse as an end in itself, and love is confused with sex. Love, for far too many men in our time, consists of sleeping with a seductive woman, one who is properly endowed with the right distribution of curves and conveniences, and one upon whom a permanent lien has been acquired through the institution of marriage.

One of the most unfortunate consequences of the emphasis on sex in our culture is that marriages are contracted by males on the basis of external attractiveness. It is a matter of prestige with men to acquire the most attractive woman for a wife, that is to say, the most externally beautiful. Males in our culture tend to marry objects rather than persons. Marriages contracted upon such a basis are not likely to be any more enduring than the curves that exercised the initial attraction, for the curves have a tendency to alter with time, while character alone endures. Is it any wonder, then, that, with the neglect of character and the emphasis on sex, one out of every three marriages in the United States should end in the divorce courts? And in the land of perpetual pubescence, California, one out of two. Think of the many more unsatisfactory marriages there must be which, for one reason or another, never reach the divorce courts. It was not merely the desire to be witty that caused George Bernard Shaw to describe contemporary marriage as in many cases nothing more than licensed prostitution. It is a correct description of innumerable contemporary marriages. Such marriages are the product of a masculine attitude that looks upon the world of women as one great harem or seraglio.

The first and most fundamental basis for any marriage is character, and not so much marrying the right person as *being* the right person. Marriages with persons of character tend to last and grow in richness. Such are not the kinds of marriages that man's present view of woman tends to encourage. Hence, man must be held responsible for the present unfortunate state of marital relationships existing between so many human beings who are tragically caught up and punished for offenses of which both are the innocent victims.

To listen to most men dilating authoritatively on the subject of women is to suffer a positive increase in one's ignorance. When men speak about women, they usually utter the most abject prejudices under the impression that they are truths pure and simple. As Oscar Wilde remarked, few things are pure, and they are seldom simple, and of all the impure and unsimple things in this world which befog and bedevil the minds of men, their ideas about women deserve to take first place. When toward the end of the fifteenth century the functionaries of the Church drew up their infamous handbook for inquisitors in dealing with women, the *Malleus Maleficarum* (1490), in answer to the question "Why a greater number of witches is found in the fragile feminine sex than among men," the answer was as simple as it was succinct. Said the authorities, "It is indeed a fact that it were idle to contradict, since it is accredited by actual experience, apart from the verbal testimony of credible witnesses" (Question 6, Part I). That, alas, is the kind of evidence on which men have always based their prejudgments of women. The myth of feminine evil has been illuminatingly examined by H. R. Hays in his book *The Dangerous Sex*.[3] It is a sorry story of hysterical fear and hatred. The story of castration and impotence fantasies, the freezing touch of the witch, vaginas equipped with teeth and snapping like turtles, phallic women and succubi, the *femme fatale*, the virgin-prostitute dichotomy, the taboos against menstrual blood, the fear of losing their male power, all testify to the deep anxiety underlying male attitudes toward women.

One of the most pervasive of myths that men have created about women is that women are possessed by sex. As a young Viennese writer in a famous book on sex and character, Otto Weininger, put it at the end of the last century, "Men possess sex; women are possessed by it." Never was the truth so madly inverted. The truth is that men are possessed by sex, while women possess it. Even among adolescents, as the Purdue study of the American teen-ager showed, for every girl who admitted "thinking about sex a good deal of the time," there were two boys who did so.[4]

Telling evidence of the male's obsession with sex is provided by the hundreds of magazines throughout the world which cater exclusively to the male's needs for sexual titillation. Where are there to be found the equivalent magazines for women such as *Playboy*, *Esquire*, *Dude*, and the like?

Biological evidence of the hormonally influenced greater aggressive sex drive of the male is curiously observed when a female suffers from a masculinizing dis-

[3] New York: G. P. Putnam's Sons, 1964
[4] H. H. Remmers and D. H. Radler, *The American Teenager* (Indianapolis: Bobbs-Merrill Co., 1957).

order produced by excessive secretion of male hormones. When this occurs the female becomes as sexually preoccupied and as aggressive as the male. Removal of the cause of the disorder (usually a tumor of the adrenal glands) results in a decline in the circulating male hormones, and she returns to her former normal balanced state.

Men, in the cultures of the Western world, not only appear to be but in fact are in a chronic state of sex irritation and are ready to indulge in intercourse with any presentable female at almost any available opportunity. This is not the case with the female, who has to be psychologically properly prepared before she is willing to accept the advances of the male. It is a tragic but significant commentary upon our culture that there are vast numbers of men who are unaware of this simple fact. This is understandable because women *seem* to be so much more preoccupied with sex than the male. The cosmetics, the beauty treatments, the hair styling, the concern with emphasizing the sexually attractive parts of the body by sexually stimulating types and arrangements of apparel, and the thousand and one other devices along the same lines calculated to have similarly stimulating effects "prove" to the male the greater sexuality of the female. This is, of course, another significant misinterpretation of the facts, again calculated to establish the inferiority of the female, for what the male fails to realize is that the female's very real preoccupation with rendering herself sexually attractive represents nothing more or less than her attempt to cater to the requirements of the male.

In January 1973 the total population of the United States was 210,000,000. Of this number 49 percent were males and 51 percent females. Thus, there are always more women of marriageable age than men. While these are mostly at the older ages, if women are to find mates, they must make themselves as attractive to males as they possibly can, and this by standards that happen to codify what feminine attractiveness is considered to be at any particular time in any particular culture. In our culture the standards are concentrated upon sexual pulchritude, and the female, therefore, adaptively attempts to fit herself to those requirements. *The behavior of women in our culture has largely been conditioned by and in response to the behavior of males toward them.* Men have placed a high premium upon sexual attractiveness; the promised dividends are high, and women, therefore, concentrate on making themselves sexually attractive. But, we repeat, it is the men who are possessed by sex, not the women. Yet there are so few men in our culture who have learned this that as a result, when women behave normally, according to their physiological state and psychological mood, men are inclined to consider them cold and frigid. And this, again, frequently leads to a disastrous denouement to what might otherwise have been a successful marriage. Unfaithfulness, extramarital relations, broken homes, divorce, and suffering on the part of everyone involved, including the children, are a few of the consequences of the false standards that men have set for women.

Men frequently condemn women for employing artificial embellishments in order to make themselves more attractive. Oh, inconsistent male, be consistent in something, and as John Donne urged, "love her who shews her great *love* to thee, in taking this pains to seem *lovely* to thee."

Even the diseases that men visit upon women, they saddle by implication upon them (venereal disease—"the disease of women").

It would be silly, if it were not also offensive, to speak in terms of drawing up a bill of attainder against men for the crimes they have committed against women.

These have been for the most part unconscious crimes, and men have no more been aware of what they were doing to women than women have, on their part, been aware of the unjustness of what was being done to them. On the whole, the motivations of men have been unconscious, and where they have not been unconscious, men's behavior toward women has been conditioned by the social heredity represented by their tradition. Men as well as women have been the victims of tradition, and as long as it continues injustice will be perpetrated. For men it will continue to remain true that divorce represents the wholly fatuous misconception that one woman is better than another. For women the general rule, under such circumstances, will continue to be: Better one man in the hand than three in the divorce court. Between the two viewpoints a wholly avoidable tragedy will remain as the precipitate; for if, under such conditions, familiarity breeds contempt, familiarity also has a way of breeding children, and these in turn will become the innocent victims of a world they never made.

We have already considered some of the social consequences of the fact that a female is capable of being pregnant and a male is not. One of the peculiar consequences of this fact is that, while there can be no doubt that a woman is having a baby, there can be a great deal of doubt about the paternity of the baby. While a man may be reasonably certain that a child is his, he cannot always be absolutely certain that it is. This fact has given rise not only to strict codes of conduct for women but also to suspicion and fear of women; for no man likes to feel betrayed by a woman, although when he chooses to betray a woman the betrayal ceases to be a betrayal and is called by some more elegant name. The double standard of sexual morality is immemorially old, as is the suspicion and fear of women. Such suspicion and fear actually revolve about the male's feeling of uncertainty about paternity, and therefore to compensate for their feeling of insecurity men have created harsh punishments and practices within which to enclose and secure the chastity of their women. The operation of infibulation, referred to in the previous chapter, is an extreme example. The medieval chastity girdle represents another example; although perhaps less brutal, it was calculated to secure the same end. In a large proportion of societies adultery was and is punished by death or payment of a heavy fine—that is, when the adultery is committed by the female. Adultery of the male has usually gone unpunished. In some societies even more horrendous punishments than death were threatened or visited upon the adulterous female—death in such cases being but the final release. The stoning to death of women taken in adultery is but one of the more gentle methods with which such women were handled. We need not go any further into the catalogue of horrors that have been visited upon women for this offense; it is sufficient to say that the penalties have been out of all proportion to its heinousness. In the civilized world of today we do somewhat better than our ancestors, though the emotional response of men to the adultery of their wives tends to be so excessive that one cannot help suspecting that the same ancient motives, at least in part, play a significant role in shaping their reactions.

The emphasis that has been placed on premarital chastity largely has its origins in male insecurities rather than in concern for the welfare of the female. The emphasis on chastity has, in effect, produced in most persons brought up in the traditions of the Western world a calculated ignorance of the facts of human growth and development. As a result, there has been a conspicuous failure to prepare for the rights, duties, and privileges of becoming a spouse and parent. The amount of damage and tragic suffering this devastating ignorance has produced is incalculable.

It is not being suggested that premarital intercourse as such is a desirable thing. It *is* being suggested that one of the by-products of the early and continued emphasis on premarital chastity has been the production of a deplorably damaging ignorance of the facts of life, of human creation, growth, and development. Such ignorance is harmful to the healthy development of the individual and therefore to the healthy development of society.

Not the biologic facts but man's social attitudes toward women—attitudes that are based upon a prejudiced misinterpretation of the facts—require revision.

4.

Who Said
"The Inferior Sex"?

THE MYTH of female inferiority is so old, and has been for so long a part of the ideas and institutions of men, that it has been generalized for almost every aspect of the female being. Is there a trait in which women have not been considered inferior to men? It would be difficult to think of one. The idea seems to be that where women are *different* from men, they are *inferior* to men. In societies wherein women have been allowed certain exclusive prerogatives, such prerogatives have not necessarily rendered them superior in those or any other respects to men—simply different, with certain rights and privileges of their own, but *not* superior to men.[1]

The myth of female inferiority has been extended not only to the mental functions but also to the physical traits and functions of the female. The lesser muscular power of the female has lent the strongest and most

[1] The reference here is to so-called matriarchal societies. Much nonsense has been written about "matriarchal societies"; modern anthropologists never use the term but refer instead to societies in which descent is reckoned in the female line as "matrilineal," and to those in which men go to live in their wives' villages as "matrilocal." No society has, in fact, ever been governed by women.

obvious kind of support to this belief. The female is "weaker" than the male. That is all men have known about the "facts," and that is all, they have felt, they needed to know. "The facts, after all, are obvious."

What countless errors, what unspeakable crimes, have been committed in the aura of the "authority" carried by such words as, "The facts, after all, are obvious." But what *is* a fact? And "after all" *what*? And what does "obvious" mean?

For most people a fact has always been something they could perceive, a thing they could grasp; but what most people have not understood is that a fact for them has been an experience they have endowed with a meaning. An experience is anything lived or undergone; a meaning is an interpretation, an adding of significance to the experience undergone. *Homo additus naturae.* And what man will add to each experience depends upon the kingdom that is within him. What human beings perceive they preconceive, in the sense that every new experience is evaluated in terms of an already existing mass of perceptions within the mind; the psychologist calls this process "apperception." They constellate ahead of experience.

Men have lived upon the earth for several million years, and for this long period of secular time they knew it to be a "fact" that the earth was flat. After all, it was "obvious." For quite as long a time it was "obvious" that the earth was a stationary body and that it was the sun that rose and set. For untold thousands of years it was believed that decaying matter generated insects. It was not until the sixteenth century that the first set of "facts" was proved to be errors, and it was not until the middle of the seventeenth century that the second "fact" was proved to be false. Most of us today would accept the same mistakes as facts were it not that it has now become part of our tradition to think otherwise. Most of us have no more proved for ourselves the facts about the solar system and the generation of insects than we have proved the "facts" we accept and subscribe to about female inferiority. "The facts, after all, are obvious."

The female is generally shorter, slighter, and muscularly less powerful than the male; these facts are obvious to everyone. The male, it is asserted, is clearly superior in these respects to the female. Let us here recall our definition of superiority in terms of the conferral of survival benefits upon the possessors of the particular traits under discussion. Do the greater size and muscular power of the male, from the biological standpoint, confer greater survival benefits upon him? We have already answered this question in the negative in the previous chapter, but let us for a moment continue with question and answer from another point of view. Do the lesser size and muscular power of the female confer lesser survival benefits upon her? The answer to these questions, on the basis of the facts, is a resounding "No!" On the contrary, the facts prove that the biological advantages are with the female.

Insofar as sheer muscular efficiency and endurance are concerned, the performance of the shorter, slighter, "weaker" female as a cross-Channel swimmer suggests that the best women can do at least as well as the best men. With respect to physical skill and staying power it may be mentioned that the English Channel Race from France to England in August 1957, in which both men and women competed, was won by a woman swimmer, Greta Anderson of Denmark, in thirteen hours and fifty-three minutes. In September 1967, Linda McGill, a twenty-one-year-old Australian, broke the women's record by swimming the Channel in nine hours twenty-five minutes, missing the men's mark by only twenty-four minutes. In September 1971, Connie Ebbelaar, a twenty-two-year-old Dutch swimming instructor, swam the

Channel from England to France in ten hours forty minutes, which was just twenty minutes away from equaling the men's record for the twenty-one-mile swim.

In a society in which there exists a great deal of repressed hostility and in which, in the last resort, its institutions are maintained by force, physical power becomes a valued social force; but this is a very different thing from claiming that it is a valuable biological trait. Civilized societies, in particular, have been characterized by a great deal of both covert and overt hostility. The quantity of violence that characterizes our contemporary societies is immense: the most widely read books of our day deal with death and disaster and crimes of violence; the theater and the motion picture carry on the tradition, and radio and television proffer, as the most staple article of diet for our children, murder, muck, and mystery, while unfunny "comics" assist in the education of violence by murdering children's minds while they are at the same time debasing the English language. War or the threat of war is almost continuously with us, and whole generations have been educated to believe that war and conflict are natural concomitants of human living. Thrilling and dangerous spectacles draw large and devoted audiences; slugging matches, miscalled "boxing," and "wrestling matches," in which no holds are barred, draw the largest followings; and now that television has brought these spectacles into the home the education in violence proceeds apace. In a land as "civilized" as the United States, a murder is committed every fifty minutes.

Though in our time we have increased the facilities for the wider education of mankind in the phenomena of violence, violence in one form or another has characterized most civilized societies for a very long time. Where violence has been traditionally resorted to as a means of settling disputes—familial, group, tribal, and intertribal—physical force becomes not only a valued trait but also a sanctioned form of behavior. For example, it is permissible to beat one's wife and one's children in most societies without in any way being penalized for doing so. Boys traditionally fight; girls do not. It should be clear that in societies that sanction a certain amount of violent behavior, men, owing to their greater muscular power, consider themselves "superior" to women in this respect, and that women readily grant them this "superiority." But it must be understood that such "superiority" is a socially conferred superiority, *not* a biological one, because the male's greater muscular power enables him to obtain certain immediate social advantages, and maintain them, over the female. If the adequate functioning and survival of the male depended upon violent conflict with the female, then there would be no question concerning the biological superiority of the male's greater muscular power; but the efficient functioning and survival of the male does *not* depend upon violent conflict with anyone else.

The greater muscular power of the male has, to a large extent, been an economically valuable trait, especially during the long period of man's history when so much of the labor expended in human societies was in the form of muscle power. Today, when machines do more than 90 percent of the work formerly done by muscle, muscular power has become an outmoded redundancy borne by its possessors at a price that exceeds any return it can yield either to them or to society.

Let us apply another test. What is the answer to the question: Which sex survives the rigors of life, whether normal or extreme, better than the other? The answer is: The female sex.

Women endure all sorts of devitalizing conditions better than men: starvation, exposure, fatigue, shock, illness, and the like. This immediately raises the question

of the alleged "weakness" of the female. Is not the female supposed to be "the weaker vessel"? "Weakness"
is a misleading word that has, in this connection, confused most people. "Feminine weakness" has generally
meant that the female is more fragile and in general less
strong than the male. But the fact is that the female is
constitutionally stronger than the male and only muscularly less powerful; she has greater stamina and lives
longer. The male pays heavily for his larger body build
and muscular power. Because his expenditure of energy
is greater than that of the female, he burns himself out
more rapidly and hence dies at an earlier age. The
metabolic rate of the male, as I have already stated, is
some 6 to 7 percent higher than that of the female.

Where, now, are the much-vaunted advantages of
larger size and muscular power? Are they biologically
fitter in any way? Are they, any longer, even socially
advantageous? The answer is that whatever benefits
men may have derived from larger size and muscular
power in the past, they have in our own time outlived
them. Today the advantages are mostly with the smaller
bodied, less muscularly powerful female.

During the last century and the early part of the
twentieth, one of the great standbys of men in arguing
the inferiority of women was the lesser absolute size and
weight of the female brain. The average weight of the
male European brain is about 1,385 grams and of the
female European brain about 1,265 grams; that is to
say, the male brain weighs, on the average, slightly
over three pounds, and the female brain, on the average,
about four ounces less. Yet on the basis of this small
difference of less than four ounces what an elaborate
mythology has been created! The four ounces have been
forgotten—if ever they were widely known—and the
difference in magnitude has been emphasized as a sub-

stantial but unstated quantity. The smaller brain of woman has always been dealt as the trump card that effectively put an end to any doubt of who had more gray matter. And since more gray matter meant more intelligence, there could be no further argument that the male was more intelligent than the female. It mattered not how often the argument was demolished by scientists. Despite the evidence repeated again and again in edition after edition of Havelock Ellis' widely circulated book *Man and Woman*, and in Amram Scheinfeld's more recent *Women and Men*, the myth seems to be as strongly entrenched as ever.

Scientific investigations on the relation between brain size and intelligence have been fairly numerous, and the general conclusion drawn from them is that *there is no relation whatever between brain size and intelligence.* The biggest human brain on record was that of an idiot; one of the smallest was that of the gifted French writer Anatole France. The idiot's brain weighed over 2,850 grams; the brain of Anatole France weighed only 1,100 grams. Within the limits of the normal range of variation of human brain weight, human beings with big brains are not characterized by greater intelligence than those with small brains.

The widespread and erroneous belief that a larger, heavier brain constitutes a criterion of higher mental faculties is understandable enough, but it happens to be false. Many prehistoric men had larger brains than contemporary man, and there is no reason to believe that they were any more intelligent than contemporary man. The elephant and the whale have larger and heavier brains than man, but no one has yet suggested that they are more intelligent than man.

An important point to understand is that a heavier or larger brain does not in itself constitute evidence of "more gray matter." As is well known, the surface area of the brain is increased by being thrown into a number of convolutions or folds, thus enabling it to occupy a much smaller volume of space than would otherwise be possible. The amount of gray matter, therefore, depends upon the number and complexity of the convolutions of the brain, and upon the complexity of the half dozen or more cellular layers of which the convoluted gray matter is composed. There is no known relationship between size of brain and number and complexity of convolutions or between size of brain and complexity of cellular organization of the brain.

Finally, in relation to total body size the female brain is at least as large, and in general larger than, that of the male! The heavier, larger male would be expected to have a slightly heavier, larger brain because all organs of the body are influenced and controlled by a general size factor and because each of the sexes possesses a brain that is proportionate to body size. However, when allowance has been made for the general size of each sex the female emerges with a slight advantage in brain size. The complete facts have been available for a century, ever since Professor T. L. W. Bischoff, the great German anatomist, published his study on the brain weight of man, *Das Hirngewicht des Menschen*, in Bonn in 1880. Since then many other scientists have independently confirmed the findings of Bischoff. As I have already mentioned, in 1894 the facts were set out in detail by Havelock Ellis in *Man and Woman*, a book that by 1934 had reached its eighth edition. But as far as many members of the reading public of the Western world are concerned, not to mention the nonreading public, it would almost seem that these studies and books need never have been published. I have never met anyone outside, and few in, scientific circles who did not believe that women had smaller brains and therefore less intelligence than men. I shall spare the reader the spectacle of nineteenth-century scientists making fools of themselves in this connection by refraining from showing how they permitted their prejudices to become involved in their "scientific" speculations. As Havelock Ellis wrote:

The history of opinion regarding the cerebral sexual difference forms a painful page in scientific annals. It is full of prejudices, assumptions, fallacies, overhasty generalizations. The unscientific have had a predilection for this subject; and men of science seem to have lost the scientific spirit when they approached the study of its seat. Many a reputation has been lost in these soft and sinuous convolutions.[2]

Lest anyone who reads these words jump to the rash conclusion that there have not been scientists within the relatively recent period to whom this comment could be applied, let me hasten to disabuse him of so generous a judgment, for there have been many. Literary men have, on the whole, not improved much, if we are to judge from what may perhaps represent an extreme case, that of the well-known German writer Max Funke, who, in his book *Are Women Human?*, stated that woman, with her small brain, must be considered a sort of "missing link," halfway between man and the anthropoid ape, and should be labeled "semi-human."

What are the facts? Bischoff, and later others, showed that the brain weight of the female in relation to the male's brain weight is as 90 to 100, whereas her body weight is to the male's only as 83 to 100. Now, if we were to raise the female's body weight to the equivalent

[2] A. & C. Black, London, 1934, pp. 119 ff.

proportion of the male, namely, 100 units, then one would have to add 17 units to the existing 90 for the female proportion of the brain to that of the male, giving us a figure of 107 for the female as compared with 100 brain units for the male. That is the proportion that most investigators have found when allowance has been made for body size. When one eliminates body fat from the weight of both sexes, the difference in brain weight in favor of the female is further increased.

Let us illustrate these facts in a simpler manner. Taking the brain weight of a large number of English, German, French, Swiss, and Russian men and women between the ages of twenty and thirty years, we find that the average brain weight of men is 1,385 grams (3 pounds and ½ ounce), while that of women is 1,265 grams (2 pounds and 12 ounces); that is to say, the absolute brain weight of man is about 120 grams (about 4 ounces) greater than that of woman. Now, if the weight of the brain is considered in relation to the weight of the body, it will be found that women possess the relatively heavier brain. The average body weight of man is about 143 pounds, while that of woman is about 121 pounds; thus the average body weight of the male is about 22 pounds greater than that of the average female. Upon calculation it will be found that while man has one ounce of brain weight for every 47 ounces of body weight, woman has one ounce of brain weight for every 43 ounces of body weight. Roughly speaking, then, the brain weight of woman constitutes about 2½ percent of the weight of the body, while the brain weight of a man is only 2 percent of his body weight.

How have the mighty fallen! But only from the rickety structure they have rather pathetically erected to make out a case for their own superior brain weight. As far as intelligence is concerned, it must again be reiterated, the facts about brain weight prove that if there were any relation (within the normal range of variation of brain weights) between these two factors the advantage would be with women; but since there is no such relation the case against women on the basis of brain weight is completely demolished—as could be the case that might be argued against the intelligence of the male on the same grounds.

So much, then, for the myth of brain weight and intelligence. Should anyone, however, for a moment think that this disposes of the brain boosters, let them prepare themselves for a shock; the brain boosters have other arguments. Granting that the female has a slight relative superiority of brain size or brain weight, what about the size, shape, and the form of the supposed seat of intelligence, the frontal lobes? We can dispose of this question rapidly: the frontal lobes are larger and more globular in the female than they are in the male. The great nineteenth-century French neurosurgeon and physical anthropologist Paul Broca, who was by no means an ardent feminist, was the first to show that if one took the cerebral hemisphere to represent 1,000, then the proportion of the frontal lobe to the hemisphere in the male is 427, whereas in the female it is 431. These findings have since been confirmed by other investigators. So much, then, for brain size and brain form.

The absurd lengths to which some alleged male scientists would go in the attempt to keep women in their "proper place" is exemplified by an Austrian writer, Dr. M. Benedikt. Since women tend to have higher foreheads than men, and since it was (erroneously) believed that a high forehead constituted evidence of high mental capacity, Dr. Benedikt maintained that in women it constituted an indication of convulsive degeneration. It is for this reason, he argued, that women instinctively attempt to conceal a high forehead by lowering their hair over it! [3]

It has been known for years that in women the cerebellum (the "little brain" beneath the "big brain," the cerebrum) is much larger than it is in males; hence nothing of this part of the brain has been heard of in the discussions concerning the relative intelligence of male and female. But there remain many other parts of the brain which have been more or less frequently cited. One is the intermediate region on the side of the brain known as the parietal area. Most investigators appear to agree that this occupies a larger area in the male than in the female. This should not be surprising, for this is the general area of sensori-motor representation, and one would expect the more muscularly active organism to have a larger parietal area. The occipital lobe (the back part of the brain), most investigators find, is of equal size in both sexes.

As for the convolutions, no one has ever found any kind of significant sexual difference either in their pattern or in their complexity; nor has anyone ever found any difference of a sexual nature in the microscopic structure of the brain. Chemical differences have been found by one group of investigators, but no one has the faintest idea what the significance of these differences may be. While it has been claimed that the female has a better blood supply to her brain, in that the combined diameters of her internal carotid and vertebral arteries in relation to total brain mass are greater than those of the male vessels, it would seem highly unlikely that this fact—if it is a fact—has any bearing upon the matter of intelligence.

We may terminate this discussion of the relationship

[3] M. Benedikt, *Kraniometrie und Kephalometrie* (Vienna, 1888), p. 125.

between brain and intelligence and its bearing upon sexual differences with the words of Havelock Ellis:

To sum up, it may be said that investigation has shown that the ancient view which credited men with a significantly larger amount of nervous tissue than women has been altogether overthrown. There is much better ground for the later view, according to which, relatively to size, the nervous superiority belongs to women.[4]

One of the earliest experiences that drew my attention, as a student, to the natural superiority of women was the observation that in the general character of the skull the female appeared to fulfill the promise, the evolutionary promise, of the child rather more significantly than did the male. This idea was by no means original with me. I can no longer recall the circumstances that led to my encountering it, though I know that the study of many thousands of skulls helped. I think it was in the pages of Ellis' *Man and Woman*, or perhaps in the pages of someone quoting Ellis, that I first grasped the full significance of the differences that struck me when comparing male and female crania.

Ellis pointed out that the infant of the great apes (gorilla, chimpanzee, and orangutan) resembles the human being much more closely than does the adult ape, for the features of the ape as it grows older become more and more animal-like. To the extent that *Homo sapiens* is ape-like, the resemblance is, on the whole, to the infant and not the adult ape. While man and woman in the course of their individual development fall somewhat away from the bountiful cranial promise of their early years, the ape in the course of its development departs very much more from the promise of its infancy

4 *Ibid.*, p. 141.

than human beings do. Humans as they grow remain more like the infant than does the ape. The skulls of an infant gorilla and of an infant human being closely resemble each other, and the skull of the infant gorilla in many respects more closely resembles that of an adult human than it does that of an adult gorilla. But as the ape grows, the skull departs more and more from its infant form, so that the adult ape skull turns out to look so unlike the infant ape skull, comparing one with the other, that one would hardly believe they belonged to the same creature.

The adult human skull preserves the promise of the infant human skull very much more than does the adult gorilla the promise of the infant gorilla skull. In other words, the adult human being is an infantilized or pedomorphic type, that is, a type that has evolved by preserving some ancestral youthful characteristics; while the adult gorilla is an aged or gerontomorphic type, that is, a type that has undergone evolutionary change as the result of accentuated development of already adult characters.

The skull of the human infant has a rather globular brain box, which relatively overshadows the small face; the bones are smooth and delicately made; there are few or no roughnesses; and the teeth are small and efficient. The more an adult skull approaches in appearance the human infant or late fetal skull, the more human it looks. *The human female skull more closely resembles that of an infant than does the male skull.* The human female, therefore, maintains the evolutionary promise of the fetal or infant skull more than does the male. The female is in the vanguard of evolution in this respect; the male falls somewhat behind.

As far as human beings are concerned, today most authorities believe that man is not only a pedomorphic type but even more a fetalized type; that is, the adult human being preserves many of the physical traits characteristic of the fetus. The infant shows these traits even more markedly than the adult; for example, in the general lack of body hair, the big head, the flatness of the face, and the flatness of the root of the nose which is associated with the so-called epicanthic eyefold that so many infants for a time exhibit. There are also the traits of the general smoothness of the bones of the skeleton, the correlated absence of eyebrow ridges and other bony ridges and tuberosities, the short legs and long trunk, and fewer hairs to the square centimeter. In other words, man is very much like a big fetus. Actually, the ethnic type whose adult members most closely preserve these fetal traits is the great major group we call the Mongoloids, and these are, perhaps, best represented by the Chinese people. To a lesser degree these traits are characteristic of all human beings, but in ethnic groups of non-Mongoloid origin they are not quite so marked at the adult stage as they are in earlier years.

Most authorities are agreed upon the important point that the infant type is the type toward which human development is directed and that human evolution has actually come about as a result of the slowing up of our development, in the womb as well as after birth. For a species having one infant at a birth and not a litter, it becomes very important for the survival of the species that the baby be well nourished and prepared before it is exposed to the dangers of birth and postnatal life. This is as true of the anthropoid apes as of man; but, as we have seen, the fetalization process becomes arrested in the ape much earlier than it does in the human. *The developmental promise of the human infant is more fully realized by the female than by the male.*

The progress of the human race has been a progress in youthfulness, in growing young rather than old. Woman exhibits that progress to a more conspicuous degree than does man, not only physically but also behaviorally. As Sir Arthur Keith has stated, "In mankind there has been a tendency to carry the joy of youth and the carefree spirit into adult life; the retention of a youthful mentality is commoner among women than among men." [5] The female, in most respects, is a more highly fetalized type than man, and adheres more closely to the line of evolutionary development indicated by the child than does the male. As Havelock Ellis wrote in *Man and Woman:*

When we have realized the position of the child in relation to evolution we can take a clearer view as to the natural position of woman. She bears the special characteristic of humanity in a higher degree than man . . . and led evolution in the matter of hairiness, simply because she is nearer the child. Her conservatism is thus compensated and justified by the fact that she represents more nearly than man the human type to which man is approximating.[6]

In more senses than one, Jesus' words have a profound meaning: "Except ye . . . become as little children, ye shall not enter into the kingdom of heaven." If human beings continue upon this earth, they will probably continue to evolve in the direction of a greater prolongation of infancy and childhood and a progressively increasing retardation of maturity.[7] Just as modern man has lost the heavily developed brow ridges and protruding jaws of his prehistoric ancestors, so it is

[5] Sir Arthur Keith, *A New Theory of Human Evolution* (London: Watts, 1948), p. 198.
[6] Ellis, p. 519.
[7] Ashley Montagu, *The Human Revolution* (New York: Bantam Books), 1967.

likely that he will continue to lose many of his present distinguishing adult characteristics. In this trend woman, as compared with man, stands in the vanguard of the evolutionary process. As Schiller wrote: "Aus der bezaubernden Anmut der Züge Leuchtet der Menschheit Vollendung und Wiege" (From the bewitching gracefulness of the features shines forth the fulfillment of humanity).[8]

[8] *Würde der Frauen* (*Dignity of Women*).

5.

"X" Doesn't Equal "Y"

WE HAVE ALREADY SEEN that there is good reason to believe that the female enjoys, on the whole, a substantial biological advantage over the male. Does there exist some biological differentiating factor that may serve to explain or possibly throw some light upon the origin and meaning of these differences? The answer is "Yes." And I do not know that anyone has made anything of a key fact that lies at the base of practically all the differences between the sexes and the biological superiority of the female to the male. I refer to the chromosomal structure of the sexes, the chromosomes being the small cellular bodies that carry the hereditary particles, or genes, which so substantially influence one's development and fate as an organism.

In the sex cells there are twenty-three chromosomes, but only one of these is a sex chromosome. There are two kinds of sex chromosomes, X and Y. Half the sperm cells carry X- and half carry Y-chromosomes. All the female ova in the female ovaries contain only X-chromosomes. When an X-bearing sperm fertilizes an ovum, the offspring is always female, XX. When a Y-bearing chromosome fertilizes an ovum, the offspring is always male, XY. It is the initial difference between the sexes in a constitutionally decisive manner. This is not to say that the sex chromosomes are eventually entirely responsible for the development of all the differences in sex characteristics; it *is* to say that the chromosomes are decisive in determining whether an organism shall develop as a male or a female. The sex chromosomes regulate the transformation of the fertilized ovum into an embryo that, during the first few weeks of development, is sexually undifferentiated, though oriented toward femaleness. Up to the end of the sixth week of embryonic development the appearance of the external genitalia is identical in the two sexes. If the embryo is a genetic male, masculinizing organizing substances will enlarge the phallus, extend the urethra along its length, and close the skin over the urogenital sinus to form the scrotum for the testes, which will later descend into it. If no masculinizing substance (i.e., testosterone, which is normally derived from the primitive gonad, the sexually indifferent organ that may develop either as an ovary or testis), the infant will develop as a female, even though a female organizing substance does not exist. This, as the distinguished experimental endocrinologist Dr. Alfred Hoet and others have suggested, indicates that the basic surviving human form is female and that masculinity is something "additional."

Under normal conditions the sex rudiments are differentially affected toward maleness or femaleness depending upon whether the chromosomal constitution (the genotype) is XY or XX. The genotype or chromosomal constitution therefore is decisive in initiating the direction of sexual development; thereafter it is a matter largely under the influence of the developing hormones secreted by the endocrine glands. The development of all bodily structures and their functions, in relation to the environment in which they develop, is set by the sex chromosomes at the time the sex rudiments and the gonads are sexually differentiated.

As Professor N. J. Berrill has written:

. . . in any case, the status of the female is never in doubt. Whoever produces eggs is essential to the future, for eggs are reproductive cells, whatever else they may be. Sperm are not so in the primary sense of the word. They serve two decidedly secondary ends—they serve to stimulate the otherwise comatose eggs to start developing, like the kiss that awakened the Sleeping Beauty, and they serve to introduce considerable variability derived from the male parent.[1]

Eggs, of course, also contribute their variability to the offspring, but eggs alone have the capacity, under certain conditions, to develop readily into grown organisms, whereas sperms lack such a capacity altogether. In all sexual species the mature organism is the egg developed, with the extra touches added, usually but not always, only when a sperm is involved.

What is the difference between an XX and an XY cell? When one looks at a body cell containing a full complement of the forty-six chromosomes [2] there will be no difficulty in recognizing the XX-sex-chromosomes because they belong with the group of quite large chromosomes. But if you pick up a body cell with the XY complement of the male, say at a magnification of two thousand diameters, then it will be seen that the Y-chromosome is among the smallest of the forty-six chromosomes. It may have the shape of a comma, the merest remnant, a wretched-looking runt compared with the well-upholstered other chromosomes! As we shall

[1] N. J. Berrill, *Worlds Without End* (New York: The Macmillan Co., 1964), pp. 155–56.
[2] All body cells contain forty-six chromosomes, the diploid number. Germ cells, those in the ovaries and testes, contain half the number, the haploid number, twenty-three chromosomes.

soon see, the Y-chromosome really is a sad affair. In
fact, its volume is only one-fifth that of an X-chromosome, and it is in that difference, and what it signifies,
that there lies part of the answer to the question: How
do the sexes get that way?

Although it has long been known that the Y-chromosome is virtually empty, it has for long been believed
that among the few genes it contained was the gene
for inducing the secretion of the masculizing hormone,
testosterone, from the gonads. It now appears that this
gene is situated not on the Y-chromosome but upon the
X-chromosome. Dr. Susumo Ohno and his colleagues at
the City of Hope Medical Center in Duarte, California,
in 1971, brought forward convincing arguments to
demonstrate that this was so. Their findings await further confirmation. If, as seems to be likely, it is shown
that femaleness is the noninduced state in the presence
of two X-chromosomes, and maleness the induced state
in the absence of one X-chromosome, the wretched
Y-chromosome will suffer its most ignominious demotion.[3]

The chromosomes, twenty-two in the haploid and
forty-four in the diploid state which are neither X nor
Y, are called "autosomes." There are twenty-two pairs of
them in the body cells, and only twenty-two single ones
in the sex cells. Each of the autosomes contains factors
that tend toward the production of femaleness. Each of
the X-chromosomes contains genes that tend toward the
production of femaleness. It used to be thought that
the Y-chromosome carries factors that were male-determining. Hence, when a Y-carrying sperm fertilizes an
ovum, the XY-chromosomes, in the presence of the
twenty-two pairs of autosomes carrying genes directed

toward femaleness, are insufficiently powerful to reduce their influence, and the result is the development of a male. On the other hand, the combination of two X-chromosomes is sufficient to overcome the influence of any possible male factors in the autosomes, and the result is a female. The X-chromosomes together have quite a pull to them; and the explanation of the biological superiority of the female lies in the male's having only one X-chromosome while the female has two. It is largely to the original X-chromosome deficiency of the male that almost all the troubles to which the male falls heir may be traced, and to the presence of two well-appointed, well-furnished X-chromosomes that the female owes her biological superiority. As a consequence of the larger size of the X-chromosome the female's cells are about 4 percent greater in chromosome volume than the male's. As Drs. J. H. Tijo and T. T. Puck, who originally determined the difference in sex-chromosome size in 1958, have remarked, the female has "a substantially richer genetic capacity than the male."

The vital importance of the X-chromosome as compared with the Y-chromosome is evident because no fertilized cell can survive long unless it contains an X-chromosome. No matter how many Y-chromosomes a cell may contain, if it does not also contain an X-chromosome it dies. Males, therefore, survive only by grace of their having been endowed by their mothers with an X-chromosome.

In birds and some insects two X-chromosomes produce a male and an XY combination produces a female, but otherwise the conditions are precisely the same as in man, except that the autosomes contain the sex genes that are strongly organized toward femaleness, whereas the X-chromosomes are strongly, and in double dose, more powerfully organized toward maleness. That it is the X-chromosome that counts is borne out by the incidence of embryo deaths, which is much greater among the female birds than among the males.

What the origin of the X- and Y-chromosomes may have been no one knows, but I find it amusing and helpful to think of the Y-chromosome as an undeveloped X-chromosome or perhaps as a remnant of an X-chromosome. It is as if in the evolution of sex a fragment at one time broke away from an X-chromosome, carrying with it some rather unfortunate genes, and thereafter in relation to the other chromosomes was helpless to prevent them from expressing themselves in the form of an incomplete female, the creature we call the male! This "just-so" story makes the male a sort of crippled female, a creature who by virtue of his having only one X-chromosome is not so well equipped biologically as the female.

But that is not the whole story. That the male is endowed with a Y-chromosome seems to put him at a greater disadvantage than if he had no Y-chromosome at all; for while the Y-chromosome may carry a few genes of some value, it also occasionally carries some that are, to say the least, unfortunate. Thus far at least four conditions have been traced to genes which sometimes occur only in the Y-chromosome and hence can be transmitted only by fathers to their sons. These are bark-like skin (ichthyosis hystrix gravior), dense hairy growth on the ears (hypertrichosis), nonpainful hard lesions of the hands and feet (keratoma dissipatum), and a form of webbing of the toes in which there is fusion of the skin between the second and third toes.

It is probable that the biological disadvantages accruing to the male are not so much due to what is in the Y-chromosome as to what is not in it. This is well exemplified by the manner in which the male inherits such a serious disorder as hemophilia (bleeder's disease). This is due to a mutant gene carried in the X-chromosome. A mutant gene is one in which a physico-chemical change of a heritable kind occurs. It has been calculated that the normal gene for blood clotting mutates to the defective hemophilia gene in one out of every hundred thousand persons of European origin in each generation. Since most hemophiliacs die before they can leave any offspring, the number of such unfortunate persons alive at any time is relatively small. Hemophilia is inherited as a single, sex-linked recessive gene, that is, a gene that is linked to the X-chromosome and that will not express itself in the presence of a normal gene on the opposite X-chromosome. When, then, an X-chromosome that carries the hemophilia gene is transmitted to a female, it is highly improbable that it will encounter another X-chromosome carrying such a gene; it is for this reason that hemophilia is of the very greatest rarity in a female. Since the survival rate to reproductive age is very low, it is obvious why females are the most usual transmitters of the hemophilia gene, and it should also be clear why females practically never exhibit the condition. The males are affected because they don't have any properties in their Y-chromosome which are capable of suppressing the action of the hemophilia gene. Women could exhibit the condition only if they inherited a hemophilia gene from their mother and another hemophilia gene from their father, and this is extremely unlikely to occur. Whether she derived the defective X-chromosome from her father or her mother, the female would not suffer from hemophilia because her normal X-chromosome would either compensate for, inhibit, or suppress the action of the hemophilia X-chromosome, and she would not become hemophiliac; but if she married a normal man and bore a number of children she would pass on the hemophilia-bearing chromosome to about half her sons and half her daughters. The girls who inherit the defective gene will show no ill effects, but the males who have received the gene may show the effects even before they are born and die of hemophilia *in utero*, or they may fall victim to the disorder at any time from birth to adult life, but exhibit the condition they will, and in the greater number of instances they will die of its effects.

The mechanism of color blindness (red-green, mostly) and its explanation are precisely the same as for hemophilia. About 4 percent of American men are completely red-green color blind, while another 4 percent are color blind in varying degrees to red-green or other colors, whereas only half of 1 percent of American women are so affected.

More than thirty serious disorders occurring in the male are known to be due to genes present in the X-chromosomes; these conditions can occur in a woman only if her father was affected and her mother carried the gene. Below are listed some of the conditions occurring more frequently in males because of sex-linked genes.

Table II. Conditions Due Largely to Sex-Linked Genes Found Mostly in Males

---

Absence of central incisor teeth

Albinism of eyes (depigmentation of eyes)

Aldrich syndrome (chronic eczema, middle-ear disease, etc.)

Agammaglobulinemia (gamma globulin deficiency in blood)

Amelogenesis imperfecta (absence of enamel of teeth)

Angiokeratoma diffusum (lesions affecting many systems of body)

Anhidrotic ectodermal dysplasia (maldevelopment of sweat glands)

Borjeson syndrome (mental deficiency, epilepsy, endocrine disorders)

Cataract, total congenital

Table II (continued)

Cataract, congenital with microcornea
Cerebellar ataxia
Cerebral sclerosis
Choroideremia
Coloboma iridis (congenital cleft of iris)
Color blindness of the red-green type
Day blindness
Deafness, congenital
Defective hair follicles
Distichiasis (double eyelashes)
Dystrophia bullosa (formation of swellings, absence of all hair, etc.)
Dyskeratosis congenita (malformation of nails, pigmentation, etc.)
Epidermal cysts (skin cysts)
Glaucoma of juvenile type (increase in fluids of eyeball)
Glucose 6-phosphate dehydrogenase deficiency
Hemophilia (bleeder's disease)
Hurler syndrome (dwarf stature, generalized disease of bone, etc.)
Hypochromic anemia
Hydrocephalus
Hypophosphatemia
Hypoparathyroidism
Hypoplasia of iris with glaucoma
Ichthyosis (scale-like skin)
Keratosis follicularis (thickening of skin, loss of hair, etc.)
Macular dystrophy
Megalocornea (enlargement of cornea of eyeball)
Menkes syndrome (retarded growth and brain degeneration, etc.)
Mental deficiency
Microcornea (diminution of cornea of eyeball)
Microphthalmia
Mitral stenosis (stricture of bicuspid valve of heart)
Myopia (short-sightedness)
Nephrogenic diabetes insipidus

Table II (concluded)

Neurohypophyseal diabetes insipidus

Night blindness

Nomadism

Nystagmus (rhythmical oscillation of eyeballs)

Oculo-cerebral-renal syndrome of Lowe (cataract, mental retardation, etc.)

Ophthalmoplegia and myopia (drooping of eyelids, absent
patellar reflexes, etc.)

Optic atrophy (wasting of eye)

Parkinsonism

Peroneal atrophy (wasting of muscles of legs)

Progressive bulbar paralysis

Progressive deafness

Pseudoglioma (membrane formation back of lens)

Pseudo-hypertrophic muscular dystrophy (weakening of muscles with growth of connective tissue in them)

Retinal detachment

Retinitis pigmentosa

Spinal ataxia

Spondylo-epiphyseal dysplasia (short stature, severe hip disease, etc.)

Thromboasthenia (defect in the thrombin, fibrin, and blood
platelet formation of the blood)

Van den Bosch syndrome (mental deficiency, skeletal deform-
ity, absence of sweat glands, etc.)

White occipital lock of hair

So much, then, for the conditions directly traceable to
genetic factors. It should by this time be quite clear
that to commence life as a male is to start off with a
handicap—a handicap that operates at every stage of
life, from conception on.

Even though male-determining sperms are produced
in the same numbers as female-determining sperms, between 120 and 150 males are conceived as compared

with 100 females. Why this should be so we do not
know, but it is a fact. The ratio at birth for American
whites is 106 males to 100 females. (The ratios vary for
different human groups, depending largely upon their
socio-economic or nutritional status.) In India the sex
ratio of boys is 98.7 to 100 girls. In other words the
poorer the nutritional conditions, the greater the le-
thality of the males; even fetal females are stronger than
fetal males. The records uniformly show that from fertilization on, the mortality rates before birth are higher
for the male than for the female fetus and that males
after birth continue to have a higher mortality rate than
females for every year of age. Within every age range,
more males die than females. For example, in 1946–48
three boy babies in the first year of life died for every
two girl babies. At about the age of twenty-one, for
every female who dies almost two males die. Thereafter,
at the age of thirty-five, 1,400 men die for every 1,000
women; at fifty-five 1,800 men die for every 1,000
women; after that the difference in death rate dimin-
ishes, though it always remains in favor of the female.

Life expectancy at birth is higher for women than for
men all over the world (except certain parts of India),
and this fact holds true for females as compared with
males for the greater part of the animal kingdom. In the
United States in 1965 life expectancy at birth for a white
female was 74.1 years, and for a white male 67.4 years;
for a nonwhite female 66.3 years, and for a nonwhite
male 61.1 years. These facts constitute further evidence
that the female is constitutionally stronger than the male.
There have been some who have argued that women live
longer than men because they don't usually work so
hard. Most men, it is urged, work harder, work longer
hours, and usually under greater strain and tension than
most women. These statements are open to question. I
am under the impression that most housewives work at

least as hard as their husbands, and under at least as great a strain.

Male fetuses do not work harder than female fetuses in the womb, yet they die more frequently before birth than female fetuses. Newborn males do not work harder than newborn females, yet they die more frequently than newborn girls. One-year-old boys do not work harder than one-year-old girls, but the boys die more frequently than the girls. And so one can go on for every age, with the difference in mortality in favor of the female.

In 1957, Francis C. Madigan, working at the University of North Carolina, published a study on the longevity of Catholic Sisters and Brothers who for many years had been living much the same kinds of lives. The same sort of disparity in their mortality rates was found to obtain as among the rest of the general population. The data were obtained on nearly 30,000 Sisters and more than 10,000 Brothers. The expectation of life at the age of fifty-four was found to be an additional 34 years for the Sisters, but only 28 years more for the Brothers, a difference in favor of the Sisters of 5½ years.

When we compare the longevity rates of bachelors with jobs with those of spinsters with jobs, we find that the advantage is again with the females. Spinsters with jobs live longer than bachelors with jobs. In 1947 the age-adjusted death rate for single men was one and one-half times that for married men, whereas among single women the death rate was only 10 percent higher than that for the married. It is an interesting fact that both among men and among women, the married have lower death rates than the single, widowed, or divorced.

A 14-nation study of the working mother conducted under the auspices of UNESCO and published in 1967 showed that women in general work longer hours and have less leisure time than men. As Professor Alexander Szalai, the project director, put it, "To summarize our

Table III. Sexual Differences in Susceptibility to Disease

MALES		FEMALES	
Diseases	Preponderance	Diseases	Preponderance
Acoustic trauma	Almost exclusively	Acromegaly	More often
Acute pancreatitis	Large majority	Arthritis deformans	4.4-1
Addison's disease	More often	Carcinoma of genitalia	3-1
Amebic dysentery	15-1	Carcinoma of gall bladder	10-1
Alcoholism	6-1	Cataract	More often
Angina pectoris	5-1	Chlorosis (anemia)	100%
Aortic disease	More often	Chorea	3-1
Appendicitis	More often	Chronic mitral endocarditis	2-1
Arteriosclerosis	2.5-1	Cleft palate	3-1
Bright's disease	2-1	Combined sclerosis	More often
Bronchial asthma	More often	Diphtheria	Slight
Brucellosis	More often	Gall stones	4-1
Cancer, buccal cavity	2-1	Goiter, exophthalmic	6 or 8-1
Cancer, G. U. tract	3-1	Hemorrhoids	Consid.
Cancer, head of pancreas	4.5-1	Hyperthyroidism	10-1
Cancer, respiratory tract	8-1	Influenza	2-1
Cancer, skin	3-1	Migraine	6-1
Cerebral hemorrhage	Greatly	Mitral stenosis	3-1
C.S. meningitis	Slight	Multiple sclerosis	More often
Childhood schizophrenia	3-1	Myxedema	6-1
Chronic glomerular nephritis	2-1	Obesity	Consid.
Cirrhosis of liver	3-1	Osteomalacia	9-1
Coronary insufficiency	30-1	Pellagra	Slight
Coronary sclerosis	25-1	Purpura haemorrhagica	4 or 5-1
Diabetes	More often	Raynaud's disease	1.5-1
Duodenal ulcer	7-1	Rheumatoid arthritis	3-1
Dupuytren's disease	3-1	Rheumatic fever	Consid.
Erb's dystrophy	More often	Scleroderma	3-1
Gastric ulcer	6-1	Tonsillitis	Slight
Gout	49-1	Varicose veins	Consid.
Harelip	2-1	Whooping cough	2-1
Harelip & Cleft Palate	More often		
Heart disease	2-1		
Hemophilia	100%		
Hepatitis	More often		

Table III (continued)

MALES		FEMALES	
Diseases	Preponderance	Diseases	Preponderance
Hernia	4–1		
Hodgkin's disease	2–1		
Hysteria	2–1		
Korsakoff's psychosis	2–1		
Leukemia	2–1		
Meningitis	More often		
Mental deficiencies	2–1		
Muscular dystrophy, Ps.h.	Almost exclusively		
Myocardial degeneration	2–1		
Myocardial infarction	7–1		
Paralysis agitans	Greatly		
Pericarditis	2–1		
Pigmentary cirrhosis	20–1		
Pineal tumors	3–1		
Pleurisy	3–1		
Pneumonia	3–1		
Poliomyelitis	Slight		
Progr. muscular paralysis	More often		
Pseudohermaphroditism	10–1		
Pyloric stenosis, congenital	5–1		
Q fever	More often		
Sciatica	Greatly		
Scurvy	Greatly		
Syringomyelia	2.3–1		
Tabes	10–1		
Thromboangiitis obliterans	96–1		
Tuberculosis	2–1		
Tularemia	More often		

findings, let's say that the last state of human bondage still persists, even if its burdens have been considerably lightened.

"More precisely, both categories of women—the working and the non-working are at a disadvantage compared with men. The working women because they are overburdened with work. The non-working women because their labors are underestimated and their existence is much more drab than that of the men."

Women are healthier than men—if by health one means the capacity to deal with germs and illness. Statistics from the public health services of various countries, and especially the United States, show that while after the age of fifteen the sickness rate is higher among females than among males, females recover from illnesses much more frequently than males do. Death from almost all causes are more frequent in males at all ages. Almost the only disorders from which women die more frequently than men are those subserving the functional systems of reproduction; namely, the reproductive tract and the endocrine glandular system.

Epilepsy has about the same incidence in both sexes, but according to the vital statistics of the Bureau of the Census the death rate from epilepsy is about 30 percent higher for men than for women.

For every female stutterer there are five male stutterers. The "stutter-type personality," who is characterized by a certain jerkiness or "stutter" of movements, as well as of speech, occurs in the ratio of eight males to one female. Word deafness, the inherited inability to understand the meaning of sounds, occurs very much more frequently in the male than in the female, and so do baldness, gout, and ulcers of the stomach. Need one go on?

The evidence is clear: From the constitutional standpoint woman is the stronger sex. The explanation of the greater constitutional strength of the female lies largely, if not entirely, in her possession of two complete X-chromosomes and the male's possession of only one. This may not be the whole explanation of the physical constitutional superiority of the female, but it is certainly scientifically the most acceptable explanation and the one least open to question.

To the unbiased student of the facts there can no longer remain any doubt of the constitutional superiority of the female.

At the present time the insurance companies charge the same insurance rates for women as for men. This hardly seems fair to women. But then when has anyone ever been fair to women? The occasions have been the exceptions. Man has projected his own weaknesses upon her and as the "muscle man" has maintained the myth of feminine weakness until the present day. But it is not woman who is weak; it is man, and in more senses than one. But the last thing on earth we want to do is to give the male a feeling of inferiority. On the other hand, we consider it a wise thing for a man to be aware of his limitations and his weaknesses, for being aware of them, he may learn how to make himself strong. The truth about the sexes will not only serve to set women free, it will also serve to set men free; for if women have been the slaves of men, men have been the slaves of their own prejudices concerning women, and this has worked no good to anyone.

6.

The Sexual Superiority of the Female

THERE EXISTS an old and widespread belief, in the societies of the Western world at least, that women are preoccupied with sex. This belief was succinctly expressed in a famous European book published at the beginning of this century, *Sex and Character* by Otto Weininger, who was in his early twenties when the book was published, and therefore an authority upon the subject, somewhat shrilly proclaimed, "Man possesses sex. Woman is possessed by it!"

Every man is, of course, an authority on sex, and every man, of course, knows that beauty parlors, permanent waves, paints, pomades, powders, women's clothes, women's arts, and practically everything about women constitute abundant testimony to their greater preoccupation with sex. Men shave, comb their hair, and wear drab clothes. They are interested in sex, of course, but their interest is as nothing compared with the interest of women in sex—and by "interest" men usually mean a preoccupation with sex. So goes the myth, a myth which Kinsey and his co-workers were the first to destroy in *Sexual Behavior in the Human Female* (W. B. Saunders, 1953); the myth was also exploded with a much smaller sample of subjects by Masters and Johnson in their book *Human Sexual Response* (Little, Brown & Co., 1966). The Kinsey workers found their women subjects to be sexually superior in every way, except in that "sexual athleticism" of a multiplicity of partners upon which the male so overcompensatingly prides himself.

Since definitions are so much more meaningful at the end of an inquiry than they can possibly be at the beginning of one, let us postpone our definition or analytic account of what we mean by "sexual superiority" until it has become so obvious to the reader in evaluating the facts for himself that the formal definition becomes doubly meaningful when he eventually comes upon it.

PSYCHOLOGIC FACTORS IN SEXUAL RESPONSE

Under the above heading the Kinsey workers reported that

In general, males are more often conditioned by their sexual experience, and by a greater variety of associated factors, than females. While there is great individual variation in this respect among both females and males, there is considerable evidence that the sexual responses and behavior of the average male are, on the whole, more often determined by the male's previous experience, by his association with objects that were connected with his previous sexual experience, by his vicarious sharing of another individual's sexual experience, and by his sympathetic reactions to the sexual responses of other individuals. The average female is less often affected by such psychologic factors. It is highly significant to find that there are evidences of such differences between the females and males of infra-human mammalian species, as well as between human females and males (pp. 649–650).

Kinsey might have said not only "infra-human mammalian species" but for almost the whole of the animal kingdom. It has long been known that in almost all sexual species of animals the female is likely to be the more quiescent and the male the more active creature. This idea was explicitly stated by Geddes and Thomson in their famous book *The Evolution of Sex* (London & New York, 1889, p. 270): "It is generally true that the males are more active, energetic, eager, passionate, and variable; the females more passive, conservative, sluggish, and stable."

Undoubtedly there is a profound phylogenetic basis for this difference between the sexes. Geddes and Thomson were the first to offer the hypothesis that the female organism is characterized by a predominance of constructive utilization of energy, by *anabolism* as compared with *katabolism* or destructive utilization of energy. This hypothesis has been widely adopted. It is a useful and an interesting hypothesis, but actually it doesn't go far enough in explaining the differences between the sexes with reference to the differences in the ends which they function to serve. The ends which both sexes serve is reproduction of the species. But reproduction of the species is not enough; the species must be maintained. And this is where the difference between the sexes expresses itself, for while it is the function of the male to produce fertilization, it is the function of the female to be fertilized and in the mammals to maintain the uterine developing organism and see it through not only to successful birth but through infancy and childhood. With comparatively few exceptions this is true of the whole animal kingdom. One may readily see, then, why the female is likely to be anabolic and the male katabolic. From the standpoint of survival the female is vastly more important biologically than is the male, and it is therefore important that she be a conserver rather than a dissipator of energy. As Tinbergen has recently pointed out in an important book,

Since the female carries the eggs for some time, often even after fertilization, and since in so many species the female takes a larger share than the male in feeding and protecting the young, she is the more valuable part of the species' capital. Also, one male can often fertilize more than one female, an additional reason why individual males are biologically less valuable than females. It is therefore not surprising that the female needs persuasion more than the male, and this may be the main reason why courtship is so often the concern of the male.[1]

The overall biological superiority of the female lies, then, in the fact that she is the more valuable part, as Tinbergen puts it, of the species' capital because she is the principal maintainer and protector of the species during children's most tender periods of development. In this fact is also to be found the explanation of the difference in sexual interest between female and male. When, then, Kinsey records these differences in psychosexual response in as great detail as he does, he is probably quite right in seeing some significant connection between such differences in human beings and similar differences in "infra-human mammalian species."

What are these psychologic factors in sexual response which Kinsey investigated? They are such factors as observing the opposite sex, nude figures, one's own sex, erotic art, genitalia, exhibitionism, movies, burlesque and floor shows, sexual activities, portrayals of sexual activities, animals in coitus, peeping and voyeurism, preferences for light or dark, fantasies concerning sex, sex dreams, diversion during coitus, stimulation by literary materials, erotic stories, writing and drawing, wall inscriptions, discussions of sex, and the like. Altogether there were thirty-three such factors investigated, and it

---

[1] N. Tinbergen, *Social Behavior in Animals* (John Wiley & Sons, 1953), p. 22.

was only in respect of three items, movies, reading romantic literature, and being bitten, that as many females or more females than males, seem to have been affected. In respect of twenty-nine of the thirty-three items fewer females than males were affected.

While there can be little doubt that social conditioning plays a considerable role in influencing patterns of sexual response, and that the male in this respect seems to be much more conditionable than the female in our culture, there can be equally little doubt that there is a profound biological difference between the sexes in this respect. The male seems to be in a chronic state of sexual irritation. The woman who, in a letter to Kinsey, described the race of males as "a herd of prancing leering goats" was not far from the truth. It is the male who is preoccupied with sex, and his preoccupation with sex in our culture at any rate is at a very superficial level. The male of the Western world is the gadfly of sex; he'll mate with virtually any woman he encounters. The female, on the other hand, is much less occupied with sex than the male. She is not in a chronic state of sexual irritation; she is not like the male in a state of continuous rut. Sexual response in the female has to be aroused, and it cannot be aroused by superficial stimulation. Sex *means* more to the female than it does to the male, and except for the highly abnormal instance of prostitution, she will not mate with any male she encounters.

These differences seem to be biologically based, and from every point of view they confer superiority upon the female—biological, moral, social, and aesthetic. The fact that these differences are biologically based does not, however, mean that the male's behavior is either excusable or unalterable. It makes it, perhaps, a little more understandable. Certainly there have been highly sexed men who have managed not to be sexual gadflies, but who have exercised their claim to being called human by respecting themselves as much as they have other people—including women.

The promiscuous male is not determined by biology but is largely the result of an inadequate education in the meaning of human relations and a puritanical conception of sex. The biological drives require satisfaction and they appear to have a much greater pressor effect and a lower excitation threshold in the male than in the female. We must learn to understand this and enable the male to order his drives in a more satisfactory manner than he has, for the most part, succeeded in doing in our culture.

For the male in our culture, the satisfaction of the sexual drive is too often identified and confused with love. The female rarely falls into such error. Yet the tragedy of sex relationships in the broad sense in our culture is that the male fails to understand what sex means to the female, and assumes that it means little more to her than it does to him. Women marry, as Kinsey points out, to establish a home and a long-term relationship with a spouse, and to have children. Men marry largely to assure themselves of an easy source for the satisfaction of their sexual needs. Though they may rationalize their needs in terms more acceptable to themselves, their wives, and their societies, "it is probable" as Kinsey states, "that few males would marry if they did not anticipate that they would have an opportunity to have coitus regularly with their wives. This is the one aspect of marriage which few males would forego" (p. 684).

From an anthropological study published a few weeks after the appearance of the Kinsey report we learn that "throughout Brazil the idea is commonly held that men do not wish to marry. Several people explained that a young man does not willingly take on the heavy responsibilities of a permanent union and renounce the pleasures of sexual adventure" (Charles Wagley, *Amazon Town*, New York, 1953, p. 169). We are not surprised—with sufficient encouragement men would everywhere take the same view. The fact is, however, that from the point of view of the biological and social health of a society such encouragement would have unfavorable results. Premarital sexual license is one thing, but the unwillingness to marry and become responsible for one's own family is quite another. It is here, too, that the pull of women to legalize illicit unions, to drag the unwilling male to the altar, has from the earliest times exercised a beneficial effect upon human society.

Women have been aware of the waywardness of the errant male, doubtless from the earliest times, and they have been caused thus to resort to every possible device in order to make themselves attractive to the male and to maintain their attractiveness in order to maintain the interest of this rovingly interested creature. Hence, the powders and the pomades, the paint and the pulchritude, and the equation in the male's mind (and in the minds of some women) of sex with love.

Unfortunately the female's much higher threshold of sexual excitability, the ease with which she is distracted even during intercourse from what is for the male the focus of all his attention, led some readers of the Kinsey report to conclude that women are not very interested in sex. This is but one example of the dangerous kind of conclusions, and utterly erroneous ones, which may be drawn from Kinsey's data. By comparison with women men are more superficially interested in sex and make up in quantitative activity what they fail to experience qualitatively. On the contrary, the female is more profoundly interested in sex, and the quality of her interest is very much more sensitively developed than that of the average male. Hence, the average male's crass sexual approaches to the female are unlikely to elicit her happiest responses.

It is, however, doubtful that with the most continuous of perfect approaches the female would, on the average, ever respond as continuously as the male does to the appropriate psychosexual stimulation. The male can, as it were, turn the faucet of sex on at a moment's notice; it takes somewhat more than a moment in the average female.

For the female, sex is a human relationship; for the male, relationships with women tend to be in terms of sex. Sex without love is no more meaningful for most women than it is for most men. Even the professional prostitute has one kind of sex for her customers and another kind for her lover. Most men, however, in their approach to sex think of *doing something to* a woman that gives themselves pleasure. These are not the words usually used; other less printable words are, and they convey the thought that the male satisfied himself on his quarry. Few women ever describe a sexual relationship with a man in such terms. Her relationship is *with* the man, and not with an adversary or victim.

In the sex relationship, as in others, women tend to humanize men. In the sex relationship what above all else they require from the male is tenderness—the tenderness which they so seldom receive. In this, too, the female, is superior to the male. The extraordinary thing is that in our culture there is a tabu on tenderness, a tabu which is sedulously taught boys, the emphasis being on "toughness." Tenderness and gentleness are looked upon as behavior fit only for a "sissy." Our men have a great deal to learn about the nature of being human, and women have a great deal to teach them. Will they succeed? I have not the least doubt that they will. It would be greatly helpful if men began to understand the problem and commenced to cooperate with women.

By virtue of her natural reticences woman is on the side of morality and the proprieties; in these respects, also, she is therefore naturally superior to the male. The female seems to come by these qualities naturally, although there can be small doubt that social influences play a considerable role in determining what she will consider moral and proper. The male will always, obviously, have a harder time behaving himself, but that he can learn to keep himself happily in check has fortunately been many times demonstrated. The proper education in human relations will enable the healthy minded male to adjust himself to himself and to other human beings as he ought. It is time that we realized that the improvement he is to make in the conduct of his sexual life will not be brought about through better "sex education" but through better education in human relations, for sex behavior is merely an aspect of human relations, of one's personal attitudes toward other human beings. It is possible that when the male of the future comes to look back upon the history of his sex he will perceive that its failure was in the realm of human relations.

Kinsey interestingly and conclusively demonstrated that while the male's sexual drives are at their peak in his early teens and shortly thereafter begin to decline, the female, on the other hand, develops her sexual urges much more slowly, and it is not till the late teens or early twenties that she really begins to mature sexually. Furthermore, Kinsey shows that the female never reaches an abrupt peak of sexuality, as does the male, but that she develops more slowly and steadily, and that while the male's sexual powers are waning hers are maintaining their steady level well into her fifties or sixties.

Men have prided themselves on their sexual athleticism, but this is as nothing compared with what women are capable of. Men may be able to muster a few orgasms at most in one session, but women can literally enjoy scores! The clitoris is a vastly more sensitive organ than the penis. Indeed, the penis has a very poor nerve supply, and compared to the clitoris it is almost without sensation. Men have tended to claim that with the menopause woman's interest in sex declines. Nothing could be further from the truth. It is at this time that most women experience a strong resurgence of sexual interest. That this is not merely mental is borne out by the fact that there is often an increase in estrogen, the female sex hormone. Hence, the menopause has been described as "the pause that refreshes." While the female's ability to experience multiple orgasms continues unfailingly into old age, the male's ability to manage more than one or two declines very markedly. In brief, the duration of the female's reproductive capacities is shorter than that of the male, but her sexual abilities are much greater and considerably outlast those of the male. It is the male sex, it should be noted, that is the impotent sex. Woman's frigidity is more often than not the product of an incompetent male.

Whatever may eventually be held accountable for these differences, the conclusion is obvious: In the duration of their sexual ardor women outlast men by a considerable margin. "There is little evidence," writes Kinsey, "of any aging in the sexual capacities of the female until late in her life" (p. 353).

It may now be apparent to the reader what we have meant by "sexual superiority" throughout this chapter. Perhaps a definition may now be acceptable on the basis of our findings. By sexual superiority we mean sexual behavior of a kind which confers survival benefits upon all who participate in it and creative benefits upon all who come within the orbit of its influence. The female enjoys this sexual superiority by fiat, as it were, of nature, but there is absolutely no reason why the male cannot learn to adjust himself harmoniously to the differences which exist between female and male, and acquire by "second nature" those controls with which the female has for the most part been endowed by nature.

Many avoidable tragedies of marriage are directly traceable to the ignorance which prevails concerning the fundamental differences that exist in the development of the sexual drives of female and male. In early marriage the male desires more coitus than his wife is ready to respond to. In later life she wants more than he is able to give, but she isn't anywhere nearly as concerned as the male is in the early years of marriage when he finds that his wife isn't as frequently responsive as he thinks she ought to be. With deeper understanding of the facts of life it will be possible for both women and men to adjust these differences in a mutually satisfactory manner. In marriage, as in all human relations, happiness is necessarily reciprocal and is found only in being given. Success in marriage does not depend so much on finding the right person, as on *being* the right person.

The biologically based differences between the sexes insofar as behavior is concerned do not need to be changed; what needs to be changed is our traditional way of dealing with it. In short, it is not human nature which should be changed, but human nurture. Here the sexes can cooperatively work together to find a better *modus vivendi* than most of us have thus far been able to work out.

It may be suggested that the best prescription for bringing about happier sex relations between the sexes is to begin with oneself, to set oneself in order as a basis for practicing good human relations, for if we are to live in a world of order we must first make order in ourselves.

7.

Are Women More Emotional Than Men?

ARE WOMEN MORE EMOTIONAL than men? Of course they are! And in this, too, they show their superiority to men. Women, unlike men, are not afraid to exhibit their feelings; they have not been trained to believe that it is unwomanly to display their emotions as men have been conditioned to believe that it is unmanly to display theirs. Women are not crippled by an inability to express their feelings when they should—as men are. As a result women are far greater realists than men. Men are the specialists in repression of feelings and what is unpleasant to them—they call it "control." Women tend to make their emotions perform the functions they exist to serve, and hence remain mentally much healthier than men.

The function of the myth that women are emotionally weaker than men has been to maintain the prejudice that while man is the supremely rational and intelligent creature, woman is the creature of her emotions. The strong silent man stands by with a stiff upper lip and a face rendered immobile by a trained incapacity for emotional expression and thus marmoreally ministers to the supposed need for sympathy and support of his frail, emotional, nervous "little woman." Is it any wonder then, that there are so many more men than women in our mental institutions, that all over the world they commit suicide so much more frequently than women, succumb to so many more nervous breakdowns than women, have four times as many stomach ulcers, and show the physical and functional disorders of emotional disturbances, in general, so much more frequently than women?

The suggestion that there are many more men than women in mental institutions seems peculiarly annoying to some men, so the statistics had better be produced. In spite of there being well over a million more women in the United States in 1951 there were 95,000 first admissions to mental hospitals for males, as compared with 76,000 for females.

An exhaustive study of the subject, by Drs. Thomas F. Pugh and Brian MacMahon, covering the years from 1922 to 1945 for first admissions in the United States, showed males far exceeded females. This is clearly seen in Table IV.

Table IV. First Admissions for Mental Illness per 100,000 per Year. Totals for All Ages

	1922	1939	1941	1942	1943	1944	1945
Male	113.8	130.6	129.3	127.9	129.3	137.1	146.5
Female	86.5	93.6	98.7	97.2	96.1	100.2	105.6

SOURCE: Thomas F. Pugh and Brian MacMahon, *Epidemiologic Findings in United States Mental Hospital Data* (Boston: Little, Brown & Co., 1962), Table 5, p. 17.

Though women *are* more emotional than men, men are emotionally weaker than women; that is, men break more easily under emotional strain than women do.

Women are emotionally stronger than men because they bend more easily and are more resilient.

Let us consider the facts.

In the first place it should be clearly understood that women are quicker to respond to stimuli, both physical and mental, than men are. In tasks involving the rapid perception of details and frequent shifts of attention, women generally excel. Such aptitude tests as the Minnesota Clerical Test reveal that only about 16 percent of male workers in the general population reach or exceed the average of female workers in checking similarities or differences in lists of names or numbers. Other investigations show a significant feminine superiority on the same test from the fifth grade through the senior year of high school. It has long been established that women possess a greater sensory acuity for color discrimination than men.

On tests measuring reaction time to a single expected stimulus, males generally do better than females, but this is not the kind of quickness of response to which I referred above. I meant quickness of response to a total complex situation, and tests reveal the superiority of the female in such situations. It is this kind of quickness of response which is often made a peg upon which to hang the myth of greater feminine emotional "weakness." Quickness is equated with nervousness or jitteriness or excitability. The fact is that in a psychophysical sense woman is more excitable, and in the physiological sense more irritable or, as Havelock Ellis put it, more affectable. Irritability is one of the criteria by which living are distinguished from nonliving things, and in a very genuine sense it requires to be said that by virtue of her greater irritability, her greater sensitivity, the female of the human species is more *alive* than the male is. Taken out of context, that might be an amusing sentence for a corner of a page in *The New Yorker*; but what it is intended to mean is that women in our culture are, on the whole, more sensitive to their environments than are men. This may be a matter of cultural conditioning, or it may have some biological basis—probably a combination of both. In any event, women do, in general, seem to be "quicker on the uptake" than men.

I do not need to cite the results of the many studies that suggest that women are more emotional than men. It is an incontestable fact; but again, whether it is a matter of cultural conditioning or biological conditioning is not easy to decide. Certainly we know that cultural factors play an enormously important role in producing differences in personality with respect to the expression of emotion as well as other traits, but the biological factor cannot be altogether dismissed. In any event, by the measure of our biologic test of superiority, how do the sexes stand concerning the expression, efficient use, and effects of emotionality?

The notion that women are emotionally weak and that men are emotionally strong is based on the same kind of reasoning as that which maintains that the female is physically inferior to the male because of the latter's greater muscular power. Trained in repression, or in the art of "schooling his emotions," as it is sometimes called, the male looks with disdain upon the female who expresses her feelings in tears and lamentations. Such behavior is in the male's estimation yet another proof of the female's general inferiority to the male; her greater emotionality is proof of her "lack of control." His own ability to control his emotions the male takes to be a natural endowment in himself which the female lacks.

All this is nonsense. In the first place it is more than questionable that women are less able to control their emotions than men. What most men—and, I fear, women, too—have overlooked is that men and women are taught to control and express different kinds of emotions. Thus, girls are taught that it is perfectly proper for them to cry but that they must never lose their tempers, and if they do, they must on no account swear: it isn't ladylike. Boys, on the contrary, are taught that it is unmanly to cry, and that while it is not desirable to fly off the handle or to cuss, well, men have always done so. Girls may not express their emotions in violent ways; girls may not fight. Boys may—and do. Nineteenth-century ladies permitted themselves to swoon or call for the smelling salts; their twentieth-century descendants are likely to swear instead, and if they call for anything it is for a stiff drink. But then these twentieth-century descendants are obviously not ladies. Twentieth-century ladies still do not curse, and if they drink, though they are today at perfect liberty to drink what they wish, they still do not drink as men do. Though it is considered "manly" for men to drink, it is not considered "womanly" for a woman to do so. Women, in fact, don't drink nearly as much as men do, and, by comparison with the rates for men, they are seldom drunk. Alcoholism and deaths from alcoholism are enormously more frequent in men than in women. Here, indeed, is a very significant difference in emotional expression, for men drink—whatever they may claim to the contrary—largely for emotional reasons, much of the time because they are unhappy; and an enormous number of them are unable to control their drinking. Whatever the reasons may be, women are able to, and do, control their drinking incomparably more successfully than men. It is interesting to observe that about the only time many men are able to cry is when they are drunk, and it may be suspected that some of them get drunk in order to be able to do so. Crying is such a good way of letting off steam. The poor things obviously don't want to be as "controlled"—by masculine standards—as they must be when they are sober.

Women don't fight, don't curse, don't lose their tempers as often as men do; they seldom get drunk and exceedingly rarely commit acts of violence against other persons. Though quicker on the uptake, they do not jump to conclusions as hastily and unconsiderately as men. Women tend to avoid the trigger responses of the male; as a result, they do not go off half-cocked as frequently as the male does. Women tend to keep their emotional balance better than men do. In short, women use their emotions a great deal more efficiently than men, and not in the "emotional" manner that men imply when they use the word disparagingly in connection with women. In this sense women are positively *less* emotional than men. In the accurate sense of the word, women are more emotional and have their emotions more effectively under control than do men. I am speaking, of course, in terms of the generality of women and men. There are exceptions to most rules in both sexes. As we shall see, from the biological and social standpoints the female orders her emotions in a manner far superior to that in which the male orders his.

Among the myths perpetuated by men is the canard that women are much more liable to fits of temperament, that they "blow their top" more easily, and are much less self-possessed. Controlled studies calculated to throw some light on this have been conducted at Oregon State College and at Columbia University. Under the same given periods of time and under the same conditions it was found that the average man lost his temper six times to the average woman's three. Studies conducted at Colgate University showed that women have more aplomb than men, and that they are less easily flustered and embarrassed and retain their self-possession longer under adverse conditions.

It is true that in the nineteenth century, women very

frequently responded to psychic shocks by swooning. The swoon served many functions: it drew attention to a lady much in need of attention; it elicited concern for her which she otherwise frequently failed to receive; and while recovering she might often obtain concessions from her "superior" mate which might not, under other conditions, be forthcoming. In other words, a capacity for swooning in the nineteenth-century female was a positive accomplishment of considerable value, a constructive use of emotion or simulated emotion which the bewildered male never really quite understood, for he always considered it a mark of inferiority in women. Weeping often served the same purpose; as a contemporary wit remarked, a woman's idea of a good cry was one that secured the desired result.

Under conditions of shock men kept a stiff upper lip, and that was supposed to be the long and short of it. After all, women were the emotional creatures. Though nineteenth-century statistics are not always reliable, they indicate that there were many mental homes, and most of them seem to have been populated largely by males. For the twentieth century, the statistics are far more accurate.

Boys as behavior problems far outnumber girls. In one study covering ten cities, the ratio of boys to girls in the problem group was four to one. Some of the types of undesirable behavior reported as occurring much more frequently in boys than in girls are truancy, destruction of property, stealing, profanity, disobedience, defiance, cruelty, bullying, and rudeness. And what is even more significant, a larger number of undesirable behavior manifestations per child were reported for boys than for girls. Boys are much less in control than girls.

A recent investigation of 579 nursery-school children revealed that, among those from two to four years of age, boys more often grab toys, attack others, rush into danger, refuse to comply, ignore requests, laugh, squeal, and jump around excessively. Girls are quieter, more frequently exhibit introverted and withdrawing behavior, such as avoiding play, staying near an adult from whom they seek praise, and "giving in too easily." All investigators agree that boys at all school ages are more quarrelsome and aggressive than girls.

In the present state of our knowledge, it is quite impossible to settle the question: Is the greater aggressiveness of the male largely or in part due to an inborn factor or is it a result of the conditioning the boy receives from his earliest age? It is quite possible that a boy, in our culture, becomes much more frustrated during the process of socialization than a girl does and that this difference already expresses itself at nursery-school age. The evidence, so far as I have been able to study it, suggests that a combination of factors, biological and cultural, is responsible for the differences in aggressiveness between male and female. I should not wish this statement to be taken to mean that the male is born with a greater amount of aggressiveness—the evidence is, to me, quite clear that no one is born aggressive at all—but rather that the evidence suggests that the male tends to be more aggressive *in part* because he has a lower threshold for frustration than does the female, tending to respond with aggressiveness where under similar conditions the female tends to exercise more control.

At the nursery-school age from three to five, boys tend to be more interested in things, while girls are more interested in personal relationships. Even at this age girls exhibit more responsibility and "motherly behavior" toward other children than do boys. Indeed, the evidence at all ages shows that the female is both socially more competent and socially more interested in human relationships than is the male. W. B. Johnson and Lewis M. Terman found that even in persons between seventy and ninety years of age happiness for the women was highly correlated with sociability, whereas in man the correlation was insignificant. In other words, in the basically most essentially desirable of human traits, namely, sociality, women are at all ages significantly superior to men. This difference and its significance will be discussed at length later in the present book; the difference is mentioned here because it gives some point to the female's manifesting from the earliest age a marked superiority in the most fundamental of all emotional qualities.

Professors Johnson and Terman, in a review of the studies that have been made on the comparative emotionality of the sexes, found that on the whole these studies agreed that the female was emotionally more "unstable" than the male.[1] This conclusion is incontestable and constitutes additional corroboration of the superiority of the female to the male. What males (even male professors) call "the emotional instability of the female" is simply an evidence of the female's superior resiliency, her possession of a mechanism that permits her to absorb the shocks of life, to tolerate the stresses and strains put upon her, much more efficiently than the male. Scheinfeld aptly offers the analogy of a car equipped with soft, resilient springs and one with harder, firmer springs:

The resilient springs (like the female's emotional make-up) would be more sensitive to all the bumps in the road, would give and vibrate more, but at the same time would take the

1 W. B. Johnson and L. W. Terman, "Some Highlights in the Literature of Psychological Sex Differences Since 1920," *Journal of Psychology,* IX (1940), 327–36.

bumps with less strain, prolonging the life of the car; the harder, more rigid springs (like the male's emotional mechanism) would not feel and respond to the minor bumps as readily but would cause more serious jolts over rough places and be more likely to result in an earlier crack-up of the car.[2]

In short, woman bends and survives, man keeps a stiff upper lip and breaks.

"Emotionally unstable" woman has been the support of "emotionally stable" man, I suspect, from the beginning of human history. Women have had to be emotionally well equipped to withstand the stresses and strains that in the course of a lifetime assault the mind and body not only of one person but at least of two. For one of the principal functions of a wife has been to serve not only as a recipient of her husband's emotional responses to life's situations but also as a scapegoat upon which her husband's unexpended aggressiveness could exhaust itself, thus offering him the psychological relief from tension in the only place he could find it—the home. Were it not for this convenient arrangement, who knows to what new heights the frequency of mental breakdown in males might not have soared? One of the age-old functions of woman has been to provide man with a sympathetic ear into which he could pour his troubles; and woman has always stood by, with the touch of her gentle hands, the calmness, strength, and encouragement of her words, to bring balm and solace and rest to the weary, puzzled, frustrated masculine soul. Woman has always been the firm rod upon which man could lean for support in time of need—and man has always needed woman. For man, because he is a male, needs a woman not only as a companion but also, upon occasion, to mother him; and a woman, because she is a female, sometimes needs to be a mother to her hus-

[2] *Op. cit.*, p. 214.

band as well as to her children. Thus it is by nature that each ministers to the unique needs of the other. But men have confused the natural complementary function and beautiful reciprocity of the sexes so that women, too, have become somewhat confused, and much pain and disorder in the world of human relations have thereby been caused. I do not mean that men never grow up to be anything except babies who are utterly dependent upon their mothers for survival, but I do mean that in their dependent relationship to their mothers they subsequently develop an interdependency in which a certain amount of reliance upon the female always fortunately remains. When such dependency functions at the adult level, it elicits those supporting responses from the female which constitute the interdependent relationship that is at the basis of all social functioning.

It is highly desirable for the sexes to understand precisely how interdependent they are; but it is even more desirable that men should realize the nature of such interdependency and make life less difficult for women, and easier for everyone concerned, by making the necessary adjustments to the facts. The sexes need each other because they are precariously dependent upon each other for their functioning as healthy human beings. Interdependency is the human state, and self-sufficiency usually winds up as insufficiency, which is the usual fate of the "self-sufficient" male. A bachelor is a poor fellow who has no one to blame but himself. Nature abhors a vacuum, but it abhors a bachelor more, and bemoans the fate of those women who (because of the incorrigible weakness of males for succumbing so much more frequently to the insults of the environment than females) fail to find a husband.

Constitutionally stronger, and more resistant to disease than men, women are much better "shock absorbers"; that is, they are better able to handle the severe emotional and psychological stresses and strains of modern life. It is a striking fact that though admission rates to mental hospitals vary, on a sexual basis, from time to time, they are, on the whole, higher for men than for women. It is also remarkable that under conditions of siege and heavy bombardment, men break down much more frequently than do women. In an important study made during World War II, *Psychological Effects of War on Citizens and Soldiers* (1942), Dr. R. D. Gillespie reported that in the heavily bombed areas of London and Kent almost 70 percent more men broke down and became psychiatric casualties than women!

Shortly after some of the heaviest bombings, the British Library of Information in New York published a bulletin entitled "Women Less Prone to Bomb Shock." It reports the results of a survey that showed that women respond to bombardment with much less emotional shock, hysteria, and psychoneurosis than do men. As Frank D. Long, who reported the survey, says:

It may be true that women are more emotional than men in romance, but they are less so in air raids. Their protective instinct for those they love is actually a shield against the nerve-shattering effects of warfare noises. They perform the job in hand with calmer deliberation than men. Men get through the job alright, but they work in a state of mental excitement—often consciously suppressed, which, in time, takes its toll.

Women also recover under psychological treatment quicker than men. Part of the treatment is the re-telling of their experiences, and it has been found that women can recall details with greater ease than men and are willing to talk about them. Repetition in this way invariably tends to rob the experience of its initial horror, which is an important aid to complete recovery of normal self-control.

Reports from the other parts of the war-scarred areas of the world are uniformly to the same effect.

Many attempts have been made to explain these facts away, but without success. It has been said that during wartime the strongest, youngest, and healthiest males are at the battlefront, that only the rejected, the sick, and the old remain behind, and that these would, "of course," tend to succumb with high frequency to the shocking effects of heavy bombings. The answer to this specious argument is that a normal distribution of physically healthy men past military age, middle-aged men and older men, constituted by far the larger number of men in the London and Kentish surveys. For concentration-camp data I know of no published figures, but it is the opinion of all those who had personal experience of such camps, and with whom I have discussed this matter, that women succumbed less frequently and withstood the rigors of the life much better than men. Here, again, it could be argued that women were better treated than men were; however, that is not the general opinion. Knowing what we now do about the constitutional differences of the sexes, one could expect women to endure such conditions of stress better than men—and they do.

One of the best indexes of resistance to emotional stress is the suicide rate. At all ages suicide rates are much higher among males than among females. In 1913 Eduard von Mayer showed that for the greater part of Europe for every female who committed suicide three to four males did so. Louis Dublin and Bessie Bunzel, in their classic study of suicide, *To Be or Not to Be* (1933), found that in the United States the suicide rate reached the extraordinary figure of ten males to three females. These authorities remark that "suicide may be called a masculine type of reaction." Actually, it becomes more masculine with age; for as age increases the ratio increases; at the older ages for every woman who takes her own life seven men do.

Most of the thirty-two governments reporting to the World Health Organization in 1950 found that suicides among men were two to five times as common as among women.

Even in suicide or attempts at suicide, men are more violent than women. Men resort to guns, hanging, and leaping from buildings, while women halfheartedly rely upon the less painful anodynes, such as sleeping pills, gas, and the like. That women generally don't want to succeed at suicide is evident: out of the 100,000 unsuccessful attempts that are annually made in the United States, 75 percent are accounted for by women. There is method in the seeming madness of many attempted suicides by females, for often the attempt is no more than a device or technique calculated to compel a desired attention.

The evidence indicates that in all times and in all societies the suicide rates have generally been significantly higher for men than for women. Women value life more than men do. Men, we have already seen, are likely to resort to more violent means of solving problems than women, and obviously this fact doesn't render them better solvers of emotional problems than women. Women look to more rational means for the solution of their problems, completely contradicting the myth that females are emotionally weak.

In the matter of who faces death with greater equanimity and genuine courage, Sergeant John Fiano, who for many years worked on death row at Sing Sing, has said that "Always, when there was more than one to be executed in one night, the weakest went first. The person with the strongest will goes last. In all my years at Sing Sing, women are always the last to go. They were much stronger emotionally than men" (J. Doyle, "Going to the Chair," *Buffalo Evening News*, 24 March 1971).

In studies of the fear of death which use self-rating scales, it has been found that women have a higher fear of death than men. This has been interpreted at its face value, but as Lester and Levene have pointed out, what may in fact have happened is that on these self-reporting scales men deny their fear of death, whereas women are more honest, or are more conscious of the fear of death than men. In an actual test, women show less fear of death perhaps because they have less fear than men, or perhaps because having faced the fear more honestly or consciously they are able to cope with the fear more adequately (David Lester & Michele Alexander, "More than One Execution: Who Goes First?" *J. Amer. Med. Assoc.* vol. 217, 1971, p. 215).

Medical men of great experience know that women bear pain much more uncomplainingly than men, and I have heard many surgeons remark that women make better patients than men. Writing in *The Listener* (London, 19 August 1966, p. 286), in an article entitled "The Relief of Pain," "A Professor of Neurology" writes, "There can be little doubt, for example, that women bear physical pain on the whole more stoically than men."

The Greeks, who were no more kind to their women than most men of other cultures have been to their women, decided that there was one disease that was peculiar to women—hysteria. They thought that the trouble began when the womb strayed from its place; hence they derived the name of the disease from the Greek word *hysteron*, meaning womb. For two thousand years women alone were, by fiat, declared capable of hysteria. It was not until 1887 that the great French alienist J. M. Charcot—one of the teachers, by the way, of Freud—showed that men, too, could suffer from hysteria. Hysteria is a disorder that is protean in the forms that it takes. It may be defined as a more or less chronic functional disorder of the mind, characterized by disturbances of the will, perversion of the inhibitory powers of consciousness, and partial arrest or hypersensitivity of the individual functions of the brain. The disorder is characterized by symptoms of the most varied character, from simple nervous instability and attacks of emotional excitement, with causeless crying or laughing, to convulsions, muscular contractions, disturbances of the circulatory system, paralysis, blindness, deafness, indeed, ailments that affect almost every organ of the body.

It has been claimed by Drs. Eli Robins, M. E. Cohen, and J. J. Purtell [3] that hysteria in men differs from hysteria in women. They believe that men always stand to gain something by falling ill with hysteria, for hysteria is an escape from something the victims are unwilling to face. Women afflicted with hysterics do not appear to have anything nearly so tangible to gain from their hysteria, according to these investigators. The men can describe their symptoms crisply, but women can never tell precisely what ails them: they babble vaguely and dramatically about pains and aches all over, and they commonly have twice as many symptoms as men. This is interesting as a differential expression of the form hysteria takes in each sex; but the reason for our discussion of hysteria here is to record that for two thousand years it was considered an exclusively feminine disease, *and that for many years the evidence of its existence in males was denied.* Apart from its being a disease "limited" to women, the condition gave quite a number of nineteenth-century medical men an opportunity to remove women's ovaries and to remove, by

[3] "Hysteria in Men," *New England Journal of Medicine*, CCXLVI (1952), 678–685. See also Ilza Veith, *Hysteria: The History of a Disease* (Chicago: University of Chicago Press, 1965).

knife or cauterization, the clitoris in an attempt to "cure" the disorder.[4] It seems difficult to believe that such drastic operations, in spite of all rationalizations by way of "explanation," were altogether motivated by a desire to benefit the patient. Hysterical symptoms in women are, as Freud so abundantly demonstrated, conversions of repressed sexual wishes into physical symptoms. Since the sexual involvement could hardly escape the attention of a perceptive nineteenth-century physician, it is not too difficult to surmise why it really was that the surgical attack upon the sexual organs was made, for nineteenth-century ladies were not supposed to be sexual at all: Men were avenging themselves upon women for having a womb and for having been ejected from it. But what is more to the point is that, while the statistics are unreliable, there is fair evidence that men are *at least* as often victims of hysteria as women, and possibly more often, for many psychiatrists of experience see at least as many male hysterics as they do female ones.

Women are generally believed to be more "nervous" than men; and, indeed, they do bite their nails and suck their thumbs more frequently as children than do boys, but this is, surely, a far superior way of expressing aggressiveness, dissatisfaction, and tension than is the boy's more violent method. The female, it has been found, beginning at a very early age, is more fearful than the male, and this may be an evidence of her more highly developed sensitivity and general superior adaptation to her environment. Fear is a basic drive that assists the organism to negotiate its way through life with the maximum chance of survival. As long as the fear responses are within normal bounds, fear is a highly desirable emotion; it keeps one from rushing in where the unafraid do not fear to tread. Lack of fear is often a

---

[4] For an illuminating discussion of these matters see Alex Comfort, *The Anxiety Makers* (New York: Dell Publishing Co., 1970).

deficiency of development which renders one heedless of dangers that more sensitive and more imaginative persons avoid. The physical courage or lack of fearfulness so often admired is generally the result of an underdeveloped imagination. I do not refer to such irrational fears as those that women have displayed, until very recently, of such creatures as mice. Such fears were very early learned and are for the most part being unrenewed by contemporary women. And yet how much was made by earlier generations of such fears as marks of the essential emotional instability of women!

Further evidences that have been cited to prove the greater "emotional weakness" of women are statements to the effect that women are gossipy, superstitious, more religious than men, and greater prevaricators; that they rely on their intuitions for their judgments, and that they are moody and temperamental.

The answer to the accusation of being gossipy is: Have you ever been a member of a men's club? Men, of course never gossip: they merely investigate rumors. Of course, women gossip. But if women were to gossip more than men, it would be perfectly understandable. Human beings are born for communication. With their children away at school and their husbands away at work, women often begin to talk to themselves; but because that isn't wholly satisfactory they talk to neighbors across the hedge or pick up the telephone and talk. Or women talk to their husbands when they arrive home and desire nothing more than to relax. In a man's view when his wife talks with her friends it is "gossip," whereas when he talks with his friends he is either "talking business" or "talking shop."

Women, on the whole, probably do talk more than men; and one of the reasons for this, I suspect, is that women find speech to be the most readily satisfactory of all tension releasers. (I wonder why it is that southern women talk, on the whole, so much more than northern women? May there not be some connection between this loquacity and the refined form of subjection of women in the South in the shapes of "chivalry," the tradition of "woman's place in the home," etc., which have been until recently, and may still be, more in force in the South than in the North?)

There have been a number of studies that indicate that women do tend to be more superstitious than men; and this is not to be wondered at, for a woman lives, in many ways, a very much more precarious psychological existence than a man. As Scheinfeld has pointed out, chance plays a much more important role in her life. When she will marry, whom she will marry, what her future is to be—these and many other questions can be settled only by chance, which is another name for Fate. No great harm can be done by subscribing to the superstitions that, so many persons reason under such conditions, *may* have something in them after all. Under conditions of a similar sort, where chance plays a considerable role, as in gambling, sports, and war, men are not one whit less superstitious than women.

Women do appear to be more religious, more idealistic, and aesthetically more interested in the relation of man to God than are men. Church attendance records, and the enthusiasm with which women throw themselves into the work of the Church, bear testimony to their religious ardor. Professor Frederick H. Lund, in a study of human beliefs, found that women "were more confident of the practicability of the Golden Rule, more assured that a democracy was the best form of government, more convinced that the world came into existence through the creative act of a divine being, more ready to question the human origin of morals." The factors that make one religious are extremely complex; possibly some of the factors that lead to the belief in superstitions are involved, but quite frankly I believe these play a very minor role. Women, it seems to me, tend to feel rather more in tune with the universe than do men, largely I suppose, because they are more sensitive to the world in which they live than men. Furthermore, while most men are able to talk with their wives and tell them their troubles, many women have no one else to talk with but their God. In God many persons often find a substitute for an inadequate earthly father or husband; such persons can the more devotedly offer their piety to a Heavenly Father as the image of one they might have had on earth. Or if life with father and his counterparts has been too much of a failure one can call on the Heavenly Mother. Consuelo Vanderbilt's mother, later Mrs. O. H. P. Belmont, the woman's suffrage leader, is said to have counseled a despairing young suffrage worker, "Call on God, my dear. She will help you." Then there is the matter of communication with the Creator, as well as with one's neighbors, in the community of the Church. Spiritual comfort can be very much more satisfying than the material comforts provided by a husband who is too busy earning a living to support the family, and occupied, when he isn't earning a living, in telling his wife what his troubles are, without leaving her any time in which to tell him hers. Everywhere it is women who remain the pillars of the Church, while men at most may be described as flying buttresses.

It will be said, "Yes, but this is an exaggeration. Women do tell their husbands their troubles, and husbands do listen." My answer is that of course there are numerous wives who have husbands who make sympathetic and helpful listeners; but for every wife who has such a husband I strongly suspect there are several who make neither sympathetic nor helpful listeners, and I suspect also that this is a factor—but certainly not the largest one—in the greater religiousness of the female.

Women, who are so much closer to the fundamental problems of life than men, are more sensitive to the needs of human beings than men. It is women who know better than anyone else that man cannot live by bread alone and that human beings are something more than slaves of the idea that men exist to earn a living and beat the other fellow to the mark. Men flatter themselves on being realists, on living in the present, and, like "practical" men, they go on repeating the errors of their predecessors. Women, who live more profoundly in the present than most men manage to do, are idealists in addition to being far better realists than men, for they see not alone the present but the coming into being of the future. They do so because they are the creators of the future—through their children. The true realists of any day are the people with vision, the visionaries, who are often described by the "practical" men as being long on hair and short on sense; the visionaries who believe in improving the world as they find it and are unwilling to accept things simply because they are; the visionaries who have the wisdom to know the difference between the things they cannot change and those they can.

Woman is a more worshipful creature than man because she understands so much more than man how much there is in the world to be worshiped, and this understanding seems clearly to be a function of her maternal role—whether she has ever had children or not. There is not the least doubt that women are by nature maternal, that men are not, and that it is the essence of the maternal attitude toward life to be sensitive to the needs of others and to retain the wonder of the miracle of creation and of the miracle of love. Such experiences and such wonderment are generative of the religious spirit. In this also, women show their superiority to men.

Lund tells us that women show more interest in the

aesthetic, the ideal, and in the mystic, and he thinks this may be due to woman's greater sensitivity, and also to training. Common experience, in our culture at least, tells us that women are more interested in the beautiful than men are. Men sometimes say, when they wish to describe the peculiar delicacy of some other man's sense of beauty, that he has a "feminine" sense of beauty. The "feminine touch" is something to which we all warmly respond. Indeed, the more closely a man's sense of beauty approaches the feminine, the less violent and the more harmonious in character he is likely to be. It is interesting to observe that during the last fifty years, with the development of the post-impressionist, non-objective schools of painting, cubism, pointillism, vorticism, and the countless other "arty" extremes, women painters have been conspicuous because, while they have progressed with the times, they have kept their aesthetic heads and not gone to the violent extremes that have characterized so many of the recent experimental schools of painting. Marie Laurencin painted exquisitely beautiful canvases, and so does Georgia O'Keeffe, in a totally different style; even that delightful "primitive," Grandma Moses, managed to avoid the contaminating influence of the machine age, painting rustic scenes with feminine ardor. The poetry and the novels of women usually show the same sensitivity to beauty, a beauty of a more loving, a more peaceful, and a more humane kind than, on the whole, characterizes the work of male writers.

In art men express something of their sense of beauty and conflict; women, on the other hand, practically never use art as a vehicle for the expression of anything but love. When women try to ape men, their aesthetic sense becomes deformed, and they vie in toughness with the male writers, let us say, of the Hemingway school. These are not the feminine writers who will endure. The women writers who will endure are those who remain true to themselves, who are admired for the virtue of their own qualities, and not for being like men. One thinks of the Brontës, Jane Austen, Mrs. Gaskell, George Eliot, Mary Webb, Willa Cather, Virginia Woolf, Pearl Buck, Doris Lessing, and many others. The humanitarianism, warmth, and moral earnestness that characterize the writings of these women grow out of a feeling for humanity based on love. It is this that gives their novels and other writings an enduring vitality and attractiveness. One may say of all these gifted women what Rosamond Lehmann wrote of three of them:

They believed, all of them, that love is of paramount significance in human affairs; that what gives life dignity and importance is the amount of love expended in personal relationships; the amount in each individual of that quality without which the human specimen, in print or out of it, is apt to look both small and dull, a predatory fragment.[5]

It is not without significance that the first two great psychological novels of Japan and of the West should have been written by women, the Lady Muraski's *The Story of Prince Genji*, completed about the year 1004, and Madame de la Fayette's *The Princess of Cleves*, which appeared in the year 1678.

Women have many firsts as innovators in literature.[6] Thus Marie of France, who flourished during the latter half of the twelfth century, is said to have invented the genre known as the Breton lay. Dame Juliana of Norwich wrote the earliest mystical prose autobiography (1342), and Dame Juliana Berners, the abbess of Sop-

---

[5] Rosamond Lehmann, "Three Giants: Charlotte Brontë, Mrs. Gaskell and George Eliot," *The New York Times Book Review*, Dec. 21, 1952, p. 5.
[6] This is a subject which has been ably dealt with by Grace Shulman in her article "Women the Inventors," *The Nation*, 11 December 1972, pp. 594–596.

well priory, near St. Albans, wrote the earliest English treatise on fishing, *The Boke of St. Albans* (1486). Margaret Cavendish, Duchess of Newcastle, wrote her autobiography (1655), and a biography of her husband (1667), which was added as an appendix to her *Observations on Experimental Philosophy*, in addition to the earliest English prose romance, *The Blazing World* (1666). This remarkable woman was also the author of *CCXI Sociable Letters*, an epistolary novel, preceding Richardson's *Pamela* (1740) in the same genre by years. The Restoration playwright, Mrs. Aphra Behn, was also the author of the famous novel *Oroonoko, or the Royal Slave* (1688), which was distinguished, among other things, for its sympathetic view of Blacks. The Gothic or horror novel was the invention of Ann Radcliffe whose *The Mysteries of Udolpho* (1794) is perhaps her most famous work. Mary Shelley's *Frankenstein* (1818) was the first science fiction story of a monster created by a scientist which subsequently kills its creator and the members of his family. As Grace Shulman points out, women were leaders in the revolution that overthrew romantic flaccidity during the twentieth century. Harriet Monroe founded *Poetry* in 1912, and Margaret Anderson founded *The Little Review* in 1915. It was a woman, Sylvia Beach, who, in 1922, had the courage to publish James Joyce's *Ulysses*.

Where tests have been made of sexual differences, it has been found that girls, in general, do better than boys on tests involving aesthetic response to color, shape, and discrimination in pictures. In tests involving the classification of pictures according to prettiness, quite small girls do better than boys. In drawing it is found that girls include more detail than boys—yet another indication of the greater sensitivity of girls to their environment than of boys.

Does anyone today really talk of women as being "born prevaricators" or "born liars"? In *Women and Men* Scheinfeld says, "The most common charge of wrongdoing which men level against women is that they are given to *lying* and *deception*." Scheinfeld thinks the charge baseless, and so do I. He considers it to be yet another example of the application of the double-standard principle: When men lie it is not the same thing as when women do. I think that there is yet another mechanism at work here, namely, *projection*. It is the easiest thing in the world to project upon others the failings we are unable to face in ourselves. The mechanism is unconscious, and hence, in its consequences, all the more real. In an investigation on lying in relation to age, conducted over a period of eight years on 151 mentally competent men and women, Dr. Nathan Masor found that the men lied about their age in 21 percent of cases compared with only 10 percent of the women. However, when the women lied they stretched the bow appreciably longer than the men.[7]

That women have had to use much tact and discretion, and employ certain artful devices in order to achieve their ends, has led some men to the conclusion that women are not "straight dealers." This is to add insult to injury, for if there have been women who were not "straight dealers"—and no one would deny that there have been many such—it is because men have forced them into the oblique approach. Most of their faults women owe to men, while men are indebted to women for most of their better qualities. Nowadays, one hears less of women's "trickiness" than one used to, for men seem to have developed a greater respect for women than their fathers had. Men often claim that women

---

[7] Nathan Masor, "The Relation of Age and Sex to Telling Lies," *Journal of the American Geriatric Society*, VII (1959), 859–861.

make fools of them. This is quite untrue. No woman ever makes a fool of a man, she merely presents him with the opportunity to realize his natural capacities.

Woman's intuition has been a favorite topic for a long time. Woman's intuition stood to her as reason stood to man and was a proof of her greater emotionality. Shakespeare, in *The Two Gentlemen of Verona*, makes Lucetta say:

> *I have no other but a woman's reason;*
> *I think him so because I think him so.*

And Shakespeare, who was himself among the most sensitively "feminine" of spirits, was a great understander and admirer of women. Indeed, as Ruskin in *Sesame and Lilies* noted many years ago, Shakespeare has no heroes; he has only heroines "The catastrophe of every play is caused always by the folly or fault of a man; the redemption, if there be any, is by the wisdom or virtue of a woman, and, failing that, there is none." Woman's intuition, as everyone knows, is a very real. faculty that most women possess in a form far more highly developed than anything the random male ever acquires. It is a kind of "sixth sense," an ability to "listen in the dark," a capacity for picking up, as it were, vibrations of very short wavelength almost as soon as they have been generated. James Stephens has put it very nicely In *The Crock of Gold* he writes, "Women and birds are able to see without turning their heads, and that is indeed a necessary provision, for they are both surrounded by enemies." Being a woman, as Joseph Conrad remarked, is a terribly difficult task, since it consists principally in dealing with men. As Helene Deutsch put it·

Woman's understanding of other people's minds, her intuition, is the result of an unconscious process through which the subjective experience of another person is made one's own by association and thus is immediately understood. The other person's subjective experience manifests itself in an external happening that is sometimes barely perceptible, but that in an intuitive person evokes by quick association a definite inner state; the conscious perception rapidly tames the inner reaction, incorporates the impression received into a harmonious series of ideas, masters the "inspirational" element, and translates it into the sober form of conscious knowledge. Since the whole process is very rapid, its second phase, that is, the intellectual elaboration, is barely perceived—everything seems to take place in the unconscious and affective element, because the conscious ingredient does not come to the fore.

What we see in intuition is not a logical concatenation of impressions; on the contrary, in each intuitive experience, the other person's mental state is emotionally and unconsciously "reexperienced," that is, felt as one's own. The ability to do this will naturally depend on one's sympathy and love for a spiritual affinity with the other person; and the extent of this spiritual affinity, for which the German language has the term *Einfühlung* (sometimes translated by "empathy"), depends on the richness of one's own emotional experiences, which underlie the "inner perception" or the ability to understand one's own feelings and psychologic relations and, by analogy, those of others.[8]

I subscribe entirely to Dr. Deutsch's admirable description of feminine intuition, and I agree when she says that women are able to identify themselves with other persons more effectively than men and that they are able to do so because of their more profound feeling for people. I do not know whether there exists a fundamental difference between the sexes in inborn potentiality for the development of intuition; I suspect there may be such a difference. I know quite a number of men who possess this quality, but they do not possess

[8] *The Psychology of Women,* I (New York: Grune & Stratton, Inc., 1944), 136–137.

it to so highly developed a degree as most women. In any event, in men the capacity seems to become progressively desensitized so that by the time they reach adult age there is, in most of them, very little of it left. Women, on the other hand, receive every assistance for its development, for sensitivity to human relations is woman's special domain.

Not so long ago men had little difficulty in believing that witchcraft was largely a feminine accomplishment. The poor blunt average male, when he first encounters woman's intuition, is astonished; it seems to him like magic. After all, he hasn't said a word or in any way indicated to her where he has been and what he had done; yet she knows, and pierces his thin disguises with an appalling certainty! How can one keep anything secret from her? Well, just as gamblers will go on believing that they can win at their gambling, so will men continue to believe that they can keep secrets from their wives. But few man have secrets that their wives do not know.

Woman's intuition is clearly a valuable trait, and its possession gives her a great advantage in the pursuit of life, liberty, and a reasonable facsimile of happiness. The great superiority it confers upon the female can no longer be disputed by anyone. To be jealous of woman's intuition, and even afraid of it, is understandable; but it is to the advantage of everyone concerned to understand that the depreciation of the good qualities of others is not the best way of acquiring them oneself.

8.

Is It True
About Women?

WHAT IS TRUTH? Statistics lie. And prejudice is all.
It's a woman driver—and if it wasn't that time, it
was the last, and the time before that, and it will almost
certainly be the next time. Why are women believed to
be bad drivers? Probably because, in the beginning,
their husbands attempted to teach them—and no near
relative, as everyone should know, should ever attempt
to teach anyone to drive. And then, of course, women at
first had less experience than men in driving. Like most
inexperienced drivers, they would not be as competent
as more competent drivers had no right to expect them
to be. But perhaps no other beam in the structure of the
male ego is so solidly mortised in place as the myth
about women drivers.

What are the facts? In August, 1938, the Keystone
Automobile Club of Pennsylvania presented facts and
figures to show that the woman driver is competent,
careful, and less liable to accidents than the male. In
that year women drivers in Pennsylvania numbered
492,934, or nearly one-fourth of the state's total of

2,086,127 registered drivers. In the six-month period
for which motor fatalities were checked, it was found
that the ratio of women drivers to fatal accidents was
1 to every 1,724 operators. On carrying the analysis further, the figures show 8.9 as many men involved as the
drivers in fatal accidents in Pennsylvania as women.

When these figures are called to the attention of those
men who automatically mutter "Woman driver" when a
car cuts in front of them, they are almost certain to
bring the retort: "Such statistics don't prove a thing.
Men drive many more miles than women, and the only
fair way to work out accident figures is on a mileage
basis. Who does the driving when the family makes long
cross-country hops, or takes off on an evening to visit
a neighbor, or goes for a Sunday spin in the country?
It's the man."

Most traffic and accident authorities—including the
Keystone Automobile Club—agree with this claim. Yet
if the mileage covered is the correct criterion, in wartime, when women obviously do a far higher percentage
of the total driving, because of the millions of men who
have left home in uniform, and because of gas rationing
that rules out cross-country hops and Sunday spins, the
accident figures for women drivers should take a jump.
But, oddly enough, in 1942 women drivers were involved in only 6.5 percent of fatal auto accidents, and
in 9.5 percent of the total number of automobile accidents. In 1943 women were still involved in only 6.5
percent of automobile fatalities, and in 10.5 percent of
all automobile accidents. By 1951 these figures had risen
to 8.0 percent and 12.0 percent respectively. In 1962
the crude death rate per 100,000 from automobile accidents was 31.5 for males and 11.2 for females. In 1966
this rose to 39.9 for males and 14.7 for females.

Information is not available on the matter of how
many more miles men normally drive than women. But

from the study of such figures as those given above, there is reason to believe that the driving abilities of women have been much underestimated. Even if a male belongs to the school of thought that believes men drive ten to twenty times more miles than women do in ordinary times, a study of such figures doesn't make the Road-Happy Harriets on our highways quite the hazards that the average American, both male and female, considers them to be.

Because men tend to drive a car as a means of self-expression or else aggressively aim it, they therefore tend to be competitive and, on occasion reckless, and are likely to take a dim view of the more careful manner in which women drive. Men tend to regard women's circumspection in driving as evidence of their lesser competence. It all depends upon the angle of vision. Most of us would prefer to ride with the careful driver rather than with the competitive one.

Women, on the whole, are thoughtful drivers. In a difficulty they will not hesitate to ask for help. Men are disinclined to do so, and rather than ask directions they would rather blunder on.

A spokesman for a large cab company that employs a number of women drivers in one of our largest cities offered the opinion that women taxi drivers have fewer accidents than men and that these are of a less serious nature than those in which men drivers are usually involved. He thought that this probably indicates that they are more cautious than men drivers and more likely to keep within the speed limit.

In 1943, at a conference on transportation held under United States Government auspices, cab companies employing women drivers gave a very favorable report on them. Half the companies reported that they did quite as well as men drivers, a quarter of the companies stated that they were safer drivers, and only 15 percent stated that they were more prone to accidents. In fairness to the men cabbies, it should be understood that men drove longer hours and that women did not work night shifts.

In August 1962, Mr. Joseph Intorre of the Institute of Public Safety at Pennsylvania State University, who at the time had been a driving instructor for over twenty-three years, stated that women in general had a great deal more respect for other cars and tricky laws than men. If they had a fault, he said, it was that they tended to be overcautious. He added that women did not tend to take risks as men do, and from this standpoint they were easier to teach. In high school driving courses girls learned as quickly as boys, and in the classroom they were often superior. Generally, he found that reflexes in both sexes were about the same.

Nearly one out of every three licensed car operators is a woman, a total of more than 37 million. To their defense came, in April 1963, the executive officers of the American Automobile Association who, according to *The New York Times* of 29 April 1963, said they were "tired of hearing long-disproved clichés" about women's driving abilities. Mr. Gilbert B. Phillips, executive vice president of the Automobile Club of New York, said that A.A.A. data showed the average woman driver to be no better and no worse than the average man.

Recognizing woman's lesser inclination to take risks, her greater patience, and her sense of responsibility, many school systems throughout the land have taken to employing women rather than men as school bus drivers.

From time to time it is a very healthy practice to hang a question mark on some of the things we take most for granted and to take another look at the facts. The myth about the woman driver is generally cited to reenforce the argument that women are too temperamental, too emotional, to make good drivers. Well, we have hung a question mark on this dearly cherished belief of the superior male, and we have found evidence that leads us to believe that the woman driver is largely a creation of the "superior" male—or rather of the male who wants to feel superior; for males, let us remember, are concerned not so much with woman's inferiority as with their own superiority.

Many men are ready to admit that, as drivers, their wives are as good as, or better than, themselves. Though they are glad to admit that their own wives are practical, wise, and levelheaded, the same men persist in thinking that the opposite is true of women as a whole. They say that women can never balance their checking accounts, that they are as blind as bats in matters where money or common sense is involved, and that shopping with them is an agony because they are indecisive and can't make up their minds. The fact is that what men so often take to be feminine indecision, and an inability to make up their minds, is in reality an inverse reflection on the trigger thinking of men. Any man who proceeds upon the theory that women do not have a hard core of practicality in their makeup is merely deceiving himself and has obviously never attempted to foist off a piece of shoddy dress goods or an inferior cut of meat on a woman shopper. Salespeople, universally, would rather see a man walk into a store than a woman. Women take time to think about what they want to buy; they are more inquisitive about the quality of the goods they purchase than men; and they are much more likely to engage in comparative shopping in an effort to obtain their money's worth. Women are aware that it is around them that the family is built and that the practical economic situation of the household is determined by the woman who runs it.

A recent survey shows that American women handle

the finances in about half the families checked. This fact should in itself constitute a sufficient commentary on the rather moth-eaten myth that women are no good at managing the finances of the household. Few men would ever have yielded the management of household finances to their wives had they not been convinced that their wives could manage better than themselves—even though there may still be some men who ungratefully rationalize away this fact with the explanation that to yield is easier. In the Life with Father era, the bills for drygoods, groceries, and clothing were supposed to be as unintelligible as Sanskrit to Mama and were paid by Papa as a matter of course. Nowadays, in millions of families, the husband hands his wife his entire paycheck, with which she pays all the household expenses and from which she gives him an allowance; or else he deducts his own allowance himself and hands his wife the remainder. Payments on insurance, rent, light, and heat are in most cases made by women, and more than 75 percent of the retail coal and oil orders are placed by women. Out of her household expense money the "financial lightweight" who shares her husband's bed and board is supposed to see to it that the laundry is checked out and checked in with a minimum loss of shirts, socks, and pajamas; that the children get to the doctor and dentist for regular examinations; and that several palatable meals are available in a continuously changing delectable variety for man, child, and dog. She is expected to keep on hand a complete supply of light bulbs, to make sure that ginger ale and soda for highballs are always on tap, to see to it that suits are always freshly pressed, and to keep herself and the children as well clothed as the family next door, where the breadwinner brings home twice as much in his pay envelope.

It is one thing for daddy to bring home a rabbit skin; it is quite another to make it stretch to fit an overgrown baby bunting of a family. If the economically infallible male took a turn at the housewife's task from time to time, he might find it an enlightening and humbling experience.

Men's stories about chuckle-headed women who think that banks use red ink because it's such a pretty color indicate what men think about women's ability to keep on the right side of the ledger. The average man has an exaggerated notion of the number of times his wife's checks rebound from the bank; he may hazard that his wife's checks bounce ten to a hundred times more frequently than his own. Interviews, however, conducted with four large banks in a city of more than two million population, bring out that women overdraw their accounts only three times as often as men. But those who are prepared to swoop with premature delight upon this not very damning evidence of female inferiority will do well to take a quick look at the figure before it dwindles. As more and more women have opened checking accounts and grown familiar with such matters, the figure has steadily shrunk. The four banks consulted agree that once women are shown a mistake in their accounts, they are much less likely than men to repeat the same error.

In the years after the turn of the century, men did the bookkeeping for the banks of the country. Nowadays, not only have women largely replaced men as our banks' bookkeepers; the same four banks mentioned above have also found that their women employees surpass men in detail work involving efficiency, such as bookkeeping and analysis. Throughout the country, more than five thousand women bank officials are acting in a supervisory capacity, and the figure is growing. Their jobs range from chairman of the board to department heads.

It is inevitable that women will play an even larger

role in banking and in the investment world, since they
are already in it up to the tops of their pocketbooks in
ownership. In 1952, according to a survey made by the
Brookings Institution, women owned almost half of all
privately owned stock in large corporations. Of the
6,490,000 owners, 3,260,000 were men and 3,230,000
women. Men owned an estimated 1,763,000,000 shares,
while women owned 1,308,000,000. The average hold-
ing per male stockholder was 160 shares, and 115 per
female. Fifteen years later (1967) these figures had
almost trebled in favor of women. Of the 18,490,000
shareowners, 9,430,000 were women and 9,060,000
men. Two-thirds of all privately owned war bonds have
a woman's name on them, as sole or co-owner, although
it is probable that men bought many of them. As of January 1967, 51 percent of individual shareholders were
women. Some 3.2 billion shares, or 17.8 percent of the
total number of shares, are registered in the names of
women. The estimated market value of these shares is
$119 billion. Sixteen percent of the total adult female
population are shareholders. Of the more than 6.4
million women shareholders more than half are housewives. In addition to women who are individual
shareowners, others have a stake in jointly owned
accounts or own shares registered in the names of stock
brokerage firms and bank nominees. Sixty-five percent
of the accounts held in mutual savings banks are held
by women. Forty percent of the titles of the 33,000,000
owner-owned homes in this country are held by women.
Eighty percent of all inheritance taxes are paid by
women. More than 40 percent of all property taxes are
paid by women. Over 80 percent of the spending of the
national income is directly controlled by women. A recent financial survey revealed that 75 percent of women
said they understood annual reports of companies in
which they own stock. Only 56 percent of the men

interviewed said they knew what such reports were all about.

During World War II a number of banks put women into jobs as substitutes for the men fighting their country's battles. The experiences of these institutions with women in positions formerly occupied exclusively by men was uniformly good, with the result that more and more women occupy higher positions in the world of banking and investment.

The boards of a number of big business organizations today have at least one woman director—a novel development in keeping with the genuine recognition that women today constitute an important factor in the whole system of American business.

The fact is that the no-account female is able to make business accounts balance at least as well as the male; and it is plainly stated by those with experience that she can usually make them balance a great deal better. Let any male who questions this statement undertake the necessary independent research for himself, and thereafter forever continue to do what he does most of the time anyway—make the big decisions and then wash his hands of the results.

9.

The Intelligence of the Sexes

A SCIENTIST IS NOT supposed to be interested in proving anything one way or the other; what he is supposed to be interested in doing is to find out what *is*, and to state it. Once stated, the "fact" is on its own. Perhaps it is this austere attitude of the scientist toward the fate of his facts which has prevented his findings concerning the intelligence of the sexes from becoming as widely known as they should be. It is extraordinary that no one has written a popular book on the subject; one would have thought that the facts relating to the most solid of entrenched myths, namely, the alleged inferior intelligence of the female, would have stimulated someone to do so. To my knowledge such a book has never been written, though there are a number of excellent works in which the relevant facts are set out in the context of a larger theme. Just as the broader significance of the sex chromosomes might have been understood much sooner if they had been discovered by a woman rather than by a man, so it may also be that because the basic work on intelligence testing was done

by males (though it has since been very largely participated in by women) it was not considered necessary to
do more than state the facts. But facts do not speak for
themselves, and unless they are given a little assistance
they have a difficult time getting established.

It was not until 1903 that the first real investigation
of the comparative intelligence of the sexes was undertaken, and at that time the investigator, Helen T.
Woolley, in *The Mental Traits of Sex*, listed less than
half a dozen previous studies of psychological sex differences. Today well over a thousand such studies are
available, but it is one thing to report the findings set
out in these studies, and quite another to say what they
mean. Fortunately, there is fairly common agreement
among scientists on the meaning of the facts. This pre-
amble is necessary because the facts obtained by intelligence tests and other tests do not speak for themselves;
indeed, when they are assumed to be speaking for themselves it is almost certain that the grossest errors of
inference will be committed because of the many concealed factors that may affect the results as reported.
For example, when one compares the intelligence scores
of elementary school boys and girls it is found that the
girls do better, on the average, than the boys. On the
other hand, the intelligence-test scores for high school
seniors are, on the average, higher for boys than for
girls. What is the meaning of these findings? Do they
mean that boys develop a higher intelligence than girls
when they enter high school years? On the face of the
scores alone this might be the conclusion, but were it to
be drawn it would be an erroneous one.

The explanation is all in favor of the girls. In practically every high school in the land there is a much more
rapid elimination of boys than girls. Boys whose school-
work is unsatisfactory drop out of school and go to work,
whereas girls tend to stay on. Furthermore, girls make a

better adjustment to the school curriculum than do boys; the slower girls make much more of an effort to master their school problems, and generally manage to pass sufficiently well to stay in school, while boys under the same conditions tend to become frustrated and give up. But such facts should put us on guard against jumping to the conclusion that high school girls are thus proven to be more intelligent than boys, or rather that a sexual difference of a biologically determined nature is involved. It *may* be that such a factor is involved, but quite obviously, or perhaps not quite so obviously, certain social factors in the differences in which girls and boys are conditioned are also to be considered.

Where especially bright children have been selected for testing, another concealed factor may enter which works to the disadvantage of girls, and that is the effect of sex stereotypes on the teachers' judgments. Since girls are generally brighter than boys at school, a girl of high intelligence may be simply regarded as a "good pupil," whereas a boy of similar intelligence may be judged as "brilliant."

Allowing for this and similar concealed and selective errors in the interpretation of the results of intelligence tests, let us, before proceeding further, first state what is to be understood by intelligence. Such a statement is not so easy as many would at first be inclined to think. There is probably not a single definition of intelligence in the psychological literature which would find universal agreement among experts.

In defining intelligence, the concepts that occur most often in the writings of psychologists are the ability to deal with abstract symbols and relationships, and the ability to adapt oneself to new situations. But these are obviously very general definitions, for there are all sorts of abstract symbols, in mathematics, music, philosophy, logic, and so on. A person may be excellent in one area of abstract symbols and poor in others. Adaptation to new situations will often depend upon a person's previous familiarity with the context of the new situation before he can adjust to it intelligently. A South American Indian from the wilds of the Chaco, however intelligent he might be in adapting himself to new situations in his home environment, would almost certainly behave like an idiot in situations completely new to him in a culture, say, such as ours. Indeed, such behavior has often been misattributed to lack of intelligence, whereas it is usually nothing more than a reflection of the cultural disorientation all of us exhibit in foreign surroundings.

Therefore it should be clear that intelligence is very closely related to experience and that it can be defined only in relation to a definite cultural setting or environmental milieu. Within our own cultural milieu, psychologists are generally agreed, intelligence in large part apparently consists of verbal ability. In fact, not altogether unseriously, intelligence could be defined, in our culture, as the capacity for verbalization which enables one to get by with fewer accomplishments than would otherwise be necessary! But, of course, it is the quality of one's capacity for verbalization and linguistic development which is important in the evolution of intelligence.

Intelligence is the ability to make the appropriately most successful response to the particular challenge of the situation. A more detailed definition of intelligence is that given by Dr. George Stoddard in his book *The Meaning of Intelligence*: [1]

Intelligence is the ability to undertake activities that are characterized by (1) difficulty, (2) complexity, (3) abstractness, (4) economy, (5) adaptiveness to a goal, (6) social value, and (7) the emergence of originals, and to maintain

[1] New York: The Macmillan Company, 1943, p. 4.

such activities under conditions that demand a concentration of energy and a resistance to emotional forces.

Possibly the only one of the attributes in this definition which requires clarification is "the emergence of originals." By this Stoddard means simply the capacity for the discovery of something new; and it is included in the definition of intelligence not because it is an inevitable outcome of high ratings in each of the other six attributes, but because of its special place at the upper end of any valid distribution of intelligence.

To what extent do males and females differ in the frequency with which they exhibit such traits?

Throughout the following presentation of the facts, let us always bear in mind the differences that exist in the social environment for males and females, the differences in what is socially expected of boys and girls, and the differences to which they must adapt themselves. Because the facts are so numerous and because it will be clearer and more helpful to the reader, I shall set those facts out in clear, brief sentences so that the reader may grasp them at a glance. Let the reader also remember that the material that goes into an intelligence test will, to a certain significant extent, determine what is meant by intelligence. Finally, I must make it quite clear that in order to obviate any suspicion of special pleading on my part I have relied entirely for the facts upon the admirable presentation of them by Professor Anne Anastasi of Fordham University and of the Psychological Corporation, in her book *Differential Psychology*.[2] In this volume, the author gives, among many other findings on individual and group differences in behavior, a quite comprehensive survey of the scientific findings relating to the intellectual functions of the sexes.

[2] Third ed. (New York: The Macmillan Company, 1958).

We may as well be prepared for what we are going to find—the cumulative effect of the repeated shock may in this way, for some males, and perhaps even for some women, be broken—namely, that with the exception of the tests for arithmetic, mathematics, mechanics, and mazes, females achieve significantly and consistently higher scores on the intelligence tests than males.

At the ages of two, three, and four the average IQ, as tested by the Kuhlmann-Binet test, is higher for girls than for boys.

From school age to adult life females obtain a significantly higher average rank on intelligence tests than men.

On tests designed for testing the intelligence of Army inductees during World War I, the Army Alpha test, New England rural women attained a significantly higher average than the men.

From infancy to adulthood the female superiority in verbal or linguistic functions is consistent and marked.

Girls of preschool age have a larger vocabulary than boys.

Girls on the average begin to talk earlier than boys.

Girls begin to use sentences earlier than boys and tend to use more words in sentences.

Girls learn to read earlier and make more rapid progress in reading than boys.

Girls have few reading difficulties compared with the great number of reading disabilities among boys.

Girls excel in speed of reading, tests of opposites, analogies, sentence completion, and story completion.

Girls do better than boys in code-learning tests.

Girls show a highly significant superiority in handling linguistic relations, as in the test requiring them to construct an artificial language. Here the subject is given a short vocabulary and a few grammatical rules, and is then required to "translate" a brief passage in English into the artificial language.

Girls learn foreign languages much more rapidly and accurately than boys, a difference that is maintained throughout life.

Girls excel in most tests of memory. They do significantly better on tests of picture memories and such tests as copying a bead chain from memory.

Girls tend to excel in logical rather than in rote memory, especially when the content of the test favors neither sex. The suggestion is that logical memory depends more upon verbal comprehension than upon anything else, hence the superior achievement on logical-memory tests of the female.

Women are characterized by a more vivid mental imagery than men.

Girls excel, on the whole, in general school achievement as measured by achievement tests and school grades.

Girls do better than boys, on the whole, in those school subjects that depend largely upon verbal ability, memory, and perceptual speed. Boys do better in those subjects that depend on numerical reasoning and spatial aptitudes, as well as in certain "information" subjects, such as history, geography, and general science.

In so far as school progress is concerned, girls are consistently more successful than boys. Girls are less frequently retarded, more frequently advanced, and promoted in larger numbers than boys.

In school grades girls consistently do better than boys, even in those subjects that favor boys.

Girls obtaining the same achievement-test scores as boys consistently had higher school grades than boys.

At the school ages, but not in the preschool age range, boys do better than girls on spatial and mechanical-aptitude tests. But a cultural factor is suspected as operative here, because boys do no better than girls in the preschool years on such tests, and it seems obvious that they depend upon the special kind of information that helps them in these tests and that is not culturally offered to or encouraged in girls. Furthermore, boys do much better in these tests than they do in the more abstract tests of spatial relations, upon which both sexes may be equally uninformed.

Boys are found to do better than girls on block counting from pictures, directional orientation, plan of search, tests of form boards, puzzle boxes, assembling objects, pencil-and-paper mazes, mechanical comprehension, arithmetic problems and arithmetic reasoning, ingenuity, and induction.

On the Army Alpha tests boys excel significantly in only three tests: arithmetic reasoning, number-series completion, and information.

In arithmetic computation girls do better than boys, but they do not do as well as boys in solving arithmetic problems and in arithmetic reasoning.

As far as intelligence scores and other indications of what we call intelligence go, the conclusion is clear: Girls do better, on the whole, on whatever it is that the intelligence tests and the other tests measure than boys. The only things in which boys do better than girls are mathematics, arithmetical reasoning, mechanical and spatial aptitudes; and the evidence indicates that cultural factors play a significant role in assisting boys to make a better showing in these areas of knowledge—for it is largely upon knowledge that, it is suspected, the superior achievement of boys, on the average, is based. That this is so is indicated by the girls' increasingly doing as well as boys on those tests in which boys formerly excelled.

It is well established that females start developing *in*

utero at a more rapid rate than males and that this acceleration in the rate of growth is maintained by the female throughout childhood and up to the age of seventeen and a half years. It has been suggested that the acceleration in physical growth in girls is also accompanied by an intellectual acceleration, in which case boys and girls of the same chronologic age groups could not be compared with one another. It would be necessary to make the comparison on the basis of psychological or developmental age rather than chronologic age. But such a procedure would seriously distort the results obtained by giving the boys an advantage of anything from a year to almost two years in training and general environmental experience. The fact is that intellectual acceleration in girls has not been directly demonstrated, and all that we know about the relationship between physical and mental factors is against the influence of physical maturation on intellectual development. Intellectual development is obviously far more dependent upon kind and quality of environmental stimulation than it is upon slight differences in physical development. And this is the critical point: What the intelligence tests measure is to a large or an appreciable extent the response that a particular person with a unique history has made to the environment in which he has been conditioned, the response he has made through the alembic of his special history of experience to the test designed to measure his "intelligence." It should, then, be obvious, that before one can pass judgment on the intelligence of one group as compared with another it is necessary to afford that group equal opportunities for the development of intelligence. It need not be emphasized here that boys and girls do not enjoy equal opportunities for the development of intelligence. Boys and girls live in different social environments; different achievements are expected of them; and they are called upon to play very different roles from earliest childhood. If girls do not have opportunities equal to boys' for the development of intelligence, neither do boys have opportunities equal to girls' for the development of intelligence. Each sex has different kinds of opportunities, and these different kinds of opportunities are not comparable; hence it is in the circumstances impossible to answer the question of the biological quality and development of the intelligence of the sexes, because the biological potentials for the development of intelligence have been so markedly and differentially influenced by the constant operation of factors of a social nature based on differences in the cultural attitudes toward the sexes.

One thing, however, is strikingly and importantly clear, and that is that intelligence, as it is defined and expected of each sex, is, on the average, something in which females of preschool and school age do better than males, with the exception of the mechanical, spatial, and mathematical reasoning tests. This does not necessarily make girls superior in intelligence to boys, but it does make them superior to boys in terms of what the intelligence tests measure, with the exceptions named. In other words, where the opportunities are afforded them and where they receive the necessary encouragements, girls generally do better than boys. Where boys receive the more favorable environmental stimulations and encouragements, they do better than girls. The evidence strongly suggests that if boys and girls received equal environmental stimulations and encouragements they would do at least equally well on whatever the intelligence tests set out to measure.

In short, the age-old myth that women are of inferior intelligence to men has, so far as the scientific evidence goes, not a leg to stand upon. Indeed, by present tests and standards of measurement girls, on the whole, do better than boys. At school they make better adjustments to conditions than boys and better satisfy the requirements of the definitions offered at the commencement of this chapter than boys do. The conclusion cannot be avoided that girls of school age are, on the whole, more intelligent than boys of school age. The fact is, whatever it may mean, that on entering school at the age of five years the average girl's mental age is two years ahead of that of the average boy!

Thus far our discussion has been focused largely on the intelligence of preschool children and children of school age because most of the intelligence tests have been carried out upon children and are both revealing and important. What now of the intelligence of adults? Here the wise and thoroughly considered words of Stoddard may be quoted:

It is futile to attempt a thorough exploration of sex differences in the later ages, in terms of the contents of present-day group or individual tests. In future, having defined intelligence with a heavy saturation in the abstract, having prepared tests with high ceilings, and with full reach to complexity and originality, all in total disregard of any found or estimated differences between the sexes, we may then apply these new tools of measurement to the sex problems indicated.[3]

Unfortunately, such tests have not yet been devised, and until they have been I think most of us will agree with Stoddard that it is futile to compare the intelligence of the sexes, on the basis of present-day intelligence tests, with the expectation of learning anything about the fundamental nature of the genetic basis of the intelligence of either sex. Such tests as have been made on adults—and there have been many—parallel the findings that have been made on school children. The same

[3] *Op. cit.*, p. 274.

holds true for males and females at college. But even so, the tests tell us quite a number of things: they tell us, for example, that there is no evidence to suggest that the female adolescent and adult are of inferior genetic intelligence to the male; they tell us that the factor of social experience is a major one in determining the development of intelligence; for as soon as the female reaches the second half of her eighteenth year she begins to evidence an increasing preoccupation with matters that are not measured by the usual tests, and she tends to become less and less interested in the content of such tests. It is at this stage that the boys begin to pull ahead on the tests; and it is at this stage that girls begin to think seriously of marriage, while boys begin to think in terms of earning a living. The one prepares for the requirements of a wife, the other for the expected requirements of a breadwinner. At this point in their lives the goals and aspirations of boys and girls are utterly different, though they are directed toward similar ends. When, therefore, the average male ends up with more information at marriage than the female at marriageable age, it is highly probable that this does not mean, as it is frequently said to mean, that the female stops growing mentally at eighteen while the male continues to do, and that this difference is due to a genetic difference between the sexes. Rather it means that while the male goes on acquiring the experience and information that intelligence tests measure, the female turns to more domestic interests that the tests do not measure.

Girls in high school and in college frequently discover the disadvantages of being "brains." Many boys tend to avoid such girls. Bright girls are, therefore, often reluctant to appear as bright as they really are. As the 1955 report of the Commission on the Education of Women, *How Fare American Women?*, showed, recent investigations indicate "that the intelligence quotients and grades of girls in high school become lower when they consider that successful academic work militates against their popularity and femininity." The same holds true for many college girls.

Summarizing the evidence, Professor Howard Moss, in his book *Comparative Psychology* (1946), writes as follows: "In human beings, it has appeared to be a universal fact that, other things being equal, there is a negligible difference between males and females in cognitive capacities. And the findings in subhuman species have been similar." If anything, the difference is in favor of the female.

As John Gibson has remarked, "Trying to evaluate the over-all intelligence of the sexes with the standard I.Q. tests is a little like trying to measure a ball of mercury with a yardstick." [4] Hence, more oblique approaches to the solution of this problem have been attempted. Humor, it has been determined, is a remarkably accurate index of intelligence. With this in mind psychologists at Wesleyan University and at Smith College investigated several hundred men and women from both institutions. They were exposed to extremely funny to utterly pointless jokes.

The results were very illuminating. The men found all the jokes much funnier than the women did, and gave them higher ratings. The women showed far greater discrimination. They were unamused by the poorer jokes, but rated the really funny ones higher than the men did. In view of the high correlation between a sense of humor and high intelligence the women in these tests scored considerably higher than the men.

Studies carried out at both Duke University and at the University of London uniformly agree that women are far better judges of character than men—yet another

[4] John E. Gibson, "Are Women Smarter Than Men?" *McCall's Magazine*, April 1953, pp. 56 ff.

evidence of women's higher problem-solving abilities.

Indeed, as Henry James remarked in his story *In the Cage*, "The cleverness of men ends where the cleverness of women begins."

At marriage, and increasingly after marriage, it should be quite obvious, the woman's intellectual interests undergo quite a change as far as many of the attributes that intelligence tests measure, whereas her husband goes on enlarging his experience and learning in those attributes. Nevertheless, married women still manage to do extremely well on such tests. With marriage and children, married women continue to grow in intelligence; and in the kind of intelligence that is of the greatest importance for the survival of the human race I think it can be shown that women far outdistance men. But before we go on to that, we must consider the matter of the intellectual and artistic creativity of women—the answer to the question: Why have there been so few great composers, artists, scientists, spiritual leaders, and great inventors and technologists among women?

10.

Women and Creativity

WHY IS IT that there have been no great musicians among women, no great logicians, philosophers, and poets? Why so few musical instrumentalists of the first rank, painters, scientists, inventors, and technologists? Have not women, from the earliest times or at least during the last few hundred years received an education in music, in painting, and been employed in the kitchens to which they have not, by their own invention, contributed (so it is usually said) a single gadget? Why, with all these opportunities, have they been so conspicuously lacking in accomplishment? Is it not for the same reason that they have been so deficient in achievement as philosophers and poets and logicians; namely, that they are lacking in the kind of genius that appears to be more abundantly distributed in the male sex?

This is a begging of the question, for it implies that there is an inborn kind of genius that probably occurs more frequently among men than among women. There exists no evidence for such an inborn limitation of the potentialities for genius of women. There is not the least reason to suspect that the genes for genius are limited to the Y-chromosome. Indeed, it is very much more likely that if such genes exist they are present on the X-chromosome, and that a female, because of her two X-chromosomes, would be likely to receive a double dose of such genes; whereas a male, because of his single X-chromosome, would receive but a single dose of them. But as far as the expression of such genes is concerned, it doesn't seem to work out that way. What, then, can be the answer?

Every dispassionate investigator of the subject has agreed that woman's lack of accomplishment cannot be due entirely to her not having had equal opportunities with men, for in many instances women have enjoyed such opportunities, as in music, the arts, philosophy, spiritual leadership, invention, and science; yet until recently their accomplishments in these fields have been far from startling. Why have there been so few outstanding representatives of the female sex in these fields?

There are many reasons.

The tradition that women are unable to do as well as men in anything requiring the use of the mind is a very ancient one.

> Seek to be good, but aim not to be great
> A woman's noblest station is retreat.

Admonishments of this kind constituted the debilitating pabulum that women were sedulously served by everyone virtually all the days of their lives. Dr. Samuel Johnson summed it up very well. "Sir," he remarked to Boswell, "a woman's preaching is like a dog's walking on his hinder legs. It is not done well; but you are surprised to find it done at all."

The truth is that if it is continually being emphasized that the individual belongs to a group that has never achieved anything and never will, and that everything ever achieved in the world has been accomplished by persons of another kind; if you tell him that it is useless to attempt to provide him with an education, or with more than the rudiments of one, because he wouldn't be able to take advantage of it; if you make laws which prevent him from owning property, as well as laws that assign him to an inferior position in the hierarchy of statuses; if you exclude him from all activities except those limited to the menial tasks of cooking, housekeeping, and executing the will of his superior in looking after children; and if you conduct yourself as if you were his natural lord and master, you will succeed—have not the least doubt of it—in convincing him that such is the natural order of things. You may, in fact, succeed to such an extent as to engender a doglike fidelity in him and an utter devotion to the principle that dog is dog and master is master—each occupying the station to which God and Nature have called him. As Rousseau aptly pointed out, "Slaves lose everything in their chains, even the desire of escaping from them; they love their servitude as the companions of Ulysses loved their brutishness."

We shall not ask the question: What does one expect of dogs other than complete loyalty? But we shall ask: What does one expect of any person under such conditions? Does one expect him to set his sights as high as the privileged ones of his society? What should he aim to achieve? At what level should his aspirations operate? What goals does he set himself? Obviously, his sights are not set because he isn't permitted the instrument; or if he is, it has no sights, and his goals and aspirations are focused almost exclusively upon pleasing his master. Since the master is so much concerned with superiority, the diminished stature of the menial—who is always at his service—is very satisfactory, especially when the menial acknowledges his inferiority in innumerable subtly flattering ways; and come weal or woe the inferior will help to maintain the *status quo*. And though the menial may sometimes experience the prickings of doubt and occasionally feel dissatisfied with his lot, so to think and feel is to partake of forbidden fruit, to eat of the tree of knowledge which is prohibited.

Masters and menials. Men and women. It is written in the first book of the Book of Books, Genesis 3:15–17, that the Lord God said unto the serpent:

And I will put enmity between thee and the woman, and between thy seed and her seed; it shall bruise thy head, and thou shalt bruise his heel.

Unto the woman he said, I will greatly multiply thy sorrow and thy conception; in sorrow thou shalt bring forth children; and thy desire shall be to thy husband, and he shall rule over thee.

And unto Adam he said, Because thou hast hearkened unto the voice of thy wife, and hast eaten of the tree, of which I commanded thee, saying, Thou shalt not eat of it: cursed is the ground for thy sake.

In I Corinthians 11:3 it is written:

And the head of the woman is the man.

And again in I Corinthians 11:7–9:

For a man indeed ought not to cover his head, forasmuch as he is the image and glory of God: but the woman is the glory of the man.

For the man is not of the woman; but the woman of the man.

Neither was the man created for the woman; but the woman for the man.

And finally:

Let your women keep silence in the churches, for it is not permitted unto them to speak; but they are commanded to be under obedience, so also saith the law.

And if they will learn anything, let them ask their husbands at home; for it is a shame for women to speak in the church.

It is said in I Timothy 2:11–15:

Let the woman learn in silence with all subjection.

But I suffer not a woman to teach, nor to usurp authority over the man, but to be in silence.

For Adam was first formed, then Eve.

And Adam was not deceived, but the woman being deceived was in the transgression.

Notwithstanding she shall be saved in childbearing, if they continue in faith and charity and holiness with sobriety.

In Ephesians 5:22–24, it is written:

Wives, submit yourselves unto your own husbands, as unto the Lord.

For the husband is the head of the wife, even as Christ is the head of the church: and he is the savior of the body.

Therefore as the church is subject unto Christ, so let the wives be to their own husbands in everything.

In I Peter 3:1, it is written:

Likewise, ye wives, be in subjection to your own husbands; that, if any obey not the word, they also may without the word be won by the conversation of the wives.

And in I Peter 3:7 the husband is enjoined to give honor to his wife, "as unto the weaker vessel."

There shall be enmity between the serpent and woman and between man and woman, and woman shall be a sorrowful creature, over whom her husband shall rule; and he shall not listen to her because she is easily deceived; but she shall learn in silence and subjection, and neither teach nor attempt to usurp authority over her husband, but remain in silence.

"Every woman," said the Fathers of the early Church, "should be ashamed of the thought that she is a woman."

Has anyone every considered what a tremendous influence these ideas from the Old and New Testaments have had upon the attitudes of men toward women in the societies that have been, in so many other respects so beneficially subjected to their influence? Of course, the ideas expressed in the passages above are much older than the Old and New Testaments; these books merely enshrined doctrines that were already old when they came to be written. The passages in Genesis were probably written some nine hundred years before those in Timothy—and in the interval no love seems to have been lost. The profound contempt for woman which these passages sanction is accentuated by the account of the undignified and irregular manner of her creation from a rib of her lord and master, whereas even the lower animals were created in a regular and decent manner. And then, to cap it all, all the misfortunes and sorrows of the human race are ascribed to the credulous folly and emotional nature, the unbridled appetite, of this lowly appanage of man—Eve, the first woman, wife, and mother.

It is with some justice that Madame de Tencin, Montesquieu's mistress, remarked, "From the way he treats us, it is easy to see that God is a man."

It is interesting to note that the biblical account of the creation of woman is paralleled by similar stories among nonliterate and other peoples in many parts of the world.

In his *Vindication of Married Life*, Martin Luther, echoing the thoughts of St. Paul, writes of that "stupid vessel," woman, over whom man must always hold power, for:

. . . man is higher and better than she; for the regiment and dominion belong to man as the head and master of the house; as St. Paul says elsewhere: Man is God's honor and God's image. Item: Man does not exist for the sake of woman, but woman exists for the sake of man and hence there shall be this difference, that a man shall love his wife but never be subject to her, but the wife shall honor and fear the husband.

Where such misogynist views of women prevail, and where women are forced to make the necessary accommodations, there is absolutely no encouragement toward achievement in the private preserve of the master. In fact, not only is such encouragement forbidden, but any attempt on the part of the menial to "usurp the authority" of the master is considered as almost equivalent to lese majesty. Women have been encouraged in the development and preservation of womanly virtues, to know their place—which is in the home—and not to aspire to be anything other than what by "Nature" they were intended to be. "And if they will learn anything, let them ask their husbands at home." The weight of this tradition and practice is still so pervasively with us that even now the vast majority of women do not come near to enjoying the same encouragements and opportunities for achievement as men. And just as it is true of intelligence, so is it true of achievement that unless one gives each sex equal opportunities there can be no means of knowing whether there are any essential inborn differences in their potentialities for achievement. On the other hand, when immemorial tradition "proves" and the present "knows" that women are inferior to men, and that women are all the things that they have traditionally been said to be, and when so many women as well as men believe these things to be true, the incentive on the part of all but a very few women is not likely to be very great.

Among the principal reasons why women do not have as many achievements to their credit as men are the following: (1) for the greater part of their history most fields of achievement have been closed to them; (2) in fields in which women were admitted they were not permitted to enter on an equal footing with men; (3) or, having been admitted, they were not encouraged to excel, were actively discouraged, or were not noticed at all. Women weren't even permitted on the stage until the seventeenth century; by far the greater proportion of them couldn't read or write when their husbands could; and when, in the nineteenth century, women first really began to express themselves through practically the only means available to them, namely, the novel, they sent their manuscripts to the publisher under a man's name—Currer Bell (Charlotte Brontë), George Sand (Aurore Dupin), George Eliot (Marian Evans) —for what woman could write? What man ever chose to send *his* manuscript to a publisher under a feminine pseudonym?

Women have been the oppressed race of the "superior" masculine world for many millennia; as an "inferior race" they have been deprived of their privileges, the right of every human being to enjoy those opportunities, equally with all other human beings, which would enable them to realize their potentialities to the optimum degree. This statement does not, of course, imply anything so idiotic as that men should be given the opportunities to give birth to babies, or that they should enjoy the freedom to suckle babies, and that women should be free to grow beards with mustaches curled at the ends—but what it *does* imply is that men and women should be given equal opportunities to realize their natural potentialities within the social milieu. These opportunities have never been fully afforded to women *or* men; but if they haven't been fully afforded to men, they have been afforded to women in an even lesser extent.

Women have always been treated as the "inferior race" by the masculine world. Everything that has been said by racists about Blacks has been said by men about women, that they have smaller brains, less intelligence, are of limited abilities, unclean, incapable of achievement, lacking in creativity, and so on. The parallel between antifeminism and race prejudice is deadly. The same impediments to self-fulfillment that have traditionally been placed in the way of Blacks have been operative for a much longer time in the case of women.

In the eighteenth century men claimed that no woman had produced anything worth while in literature, with the possible exception of Sappho. Since women had failed to do so up to that time, it was argued, it was a fair assumption that they would never do so. But within the first half of the nineteenth century they were to be proven wrong, for women writers of genius commenced the break into the literary world that took it by storm: Jane Austen, Elizabeth Gaskell, Charlotte Brontë, Emily Brontë, George Eliot, George Sand, and Elizabeth Barrett Browning. In more recent times such distinguished writers as Emily Dickinson, Mary Webb, Virginia Woolf, Edith Wharton, Willa Cather, Edna St. Vincent Millay, Pearl Buck, Doris Lessing, Sigrid Undset, Selma Lagerlöf, Grazia Deledda, Mary McCarthy, and many others have appeared. No one any longer doubts that women can write, and that what they have to say is worth listening to.

Nevertheless arguments are still heard to the effect that relatively few women have achieved greatness in the fields in which men have excelled.

There has been only one great woman scientist, it is said, Mme. Curie. This is not true. There have been a half-dozen women Nobel prizewinners since Mme. Curie. Even at this late date how many women enjoy the same opportunities as men to become great scientists? What chance does a woman stand to obtain even an instructorship in any of the science departments in our colleges and universities?

Although in all doctoral fields, women receiving the doctorate are brighter than their male counterparts, and there are no differences in their productivity, and their durability on the job is greater than that of men—even though their rate of promotion and their salaries are less—and absenteeism is no higher than that of men, hiring departments give the edge to men when applications are identical, except for sex.[1]

As the editor of *Science*, Philip H. Abelson, stated in an editorial, "There has been massive discrimination against women in academia." And he points out that while only about 2 percent of women are full professors in our major universities, women obtain 12 percent of the doctorates annually awarded.[2]

For centuries it was quite impossible for women even to think of entering into activities which were regarded as the exclusive prerogative of the male. It was taken for granted that women could never succeed in any "male" occupation. Since the occupations were by definition "male," it was hardly conceivable that any woman would even dream of entering them.

Even though the citadels of male privilege have to some extent been breached, full equality has yet to be

[1] Susan M. Ervin-Tripp, "Women With Ph.D.'s." *Science*, 174, 1971, 1281

[2] Philip H. Abelson, "Women in Academia," *Science*, 175, 1972, 127. See also Arie Y. Lewin and Linda Duchan, "Women in Academia," *Science*, 173, 1972, 892–895.

See also Grace Rubin-Rabson, "Women and the Professions," *Science*, 176, 1972, 1183–1184; Florance Moog, "Women, Students, and Tenure," *Science*, 174, 1971, 983. Deborah Shapley, "University Women's Rights: Whose Feet are Dragging?" *Science*, 175, 1972, 151–154.

achieved. Discrimination against women is still a factor very much to be reckoned with.

Music and painting are most frequently cited as two arts in which women have been engaged for several hundred years. During that time there have been numerous male musicians of genius, and not a single female composer of any note, and few instrumentalists of the first quality. If it is said that there was no incentive for women to excel in these arts, one may ask whether there was any incentive for them to excel in singing, for there have been many great women singers, as all the world knows.

Ever since the first mother sang her baby to sleep, song and chant have been universally associated with women. Lullabies and lieder, dirges and laments, have from the earliest times naturally been a preserve of women. The first songs that the male learns are most often learned from women. There is, therefore, a long and acceptable tradition of woman as a songstress. Her voice can produce effects that no man's can, and these are sweet and pleasing and colorful. Hence, we may be reasonably sure that song is one natural capacity in which women have received encouragement from the earliest times, and the nurturing of women singers in our culture may represent the persisting practice of an immemorial tradition.

In musical composition and the public performance of music, however, the aspect is altered. Sophie Drinker, in her book *Music and Women*,[3] has shown that women have not been musically creative in our culture owing to the historical causes that brought about a nonpermissive environment for the woman musician. The music of our culture was originally indissolubly bound to organized religion and limited to church use. Women were offi-

[3] New York: Coward-McCann, Inc., 1948.

cially debarred from playing any part in the religious ceremony and so became automatically cut off from the main source and inspiration for original creativity in music. Nuns, who occupied a specific place in the hierarchy, composed only liturgical and extraliturgical music and then only within the limits of the few opportunities offered them. Mrs. Drinker points out:

When men and women freed themselves from the heavy restrictions placed upon the free use of music by the churchmen and began to use music apart from ritual and liturgy, women were *theoretically* able to function again as musicians. But the leaders in music were still those connected with, or employed by, religious officials, and according to the established custom of over a thousand years, were all men. Effective musical education and training were still in the church. Since the supply of men musicians was sufficient, women were not in demand but were expected rather to patronize and perform men's music. Furthermore, even though ecclesiastical authority waned, authority in church, state, educational system, and home remained largely in the hands of men. And it was an authority reinforced by the religion that women were spiritually and intellectually inferior to men.[4]

Whoever would have thought of employing a female court musician? What woman would have dared offer herself in such a capacity? Does anyone today look with greater favor upon a female radio announcer than they do upon a female orchestral conductor? Why are there no popular female jazz bands? Is it because the level of musical performance is so high that no woman could achieve it? One may doubt whether there would be many persons who would care to sustain the argument. Certainly no one would who has heard Phil Spitalny's all-girl orchestra. Numberless women have played and do play every one of the instruments one finds in the

[4] Ibid., p. 295.

largest orchestras, and play them well. The fact is that a jazz orchestra of women simply doesn't constitute the right *décor*. Women prefer all-male bands, but they have no objection to the girl often attached to such orchestras, who sings a few "numbers." Nevertheless, a few all-women symphonic orchestras have appeared and braved the entrenched prejudices of the sexes. Izler Solomon, the first conductor of the first all-woman symphonic orchestra to appear regularly on the air, in a statement published in *The New York Times* of September 29, 1940, said: "It is perfect nonsense to say that women are inferior to men in the world of music. . . . In many instances they are better than men. Women are more sensitive and are apt to have a finer perceptive reaction to phrasing." In the same newspaper, for October 26, 1946, Hans Kindler said of women musicians: "Their ability and enthusiasm constitute an added stimulant for the male performers . . . they were a veritable godsend to most conductors during the war years. The National Symphony has re-engaged its fifteen women players." And Leopold Stokowski said, "I find that women are equally as talented as men." On the other hand, Sir Thomas Beecham announced that "women ruin music." He said, "If the ladies are ill-favored the men do not want to play next to them, and if they are well-favored, they can't." José Iturbi has held that women can never be "great musicians." When he was associated with the Rochester Symphony Orchestra, he refused to accept girl graduates from the Eastman School of Music as players in the orchestra.

Compared with the male, the female still finds it difficult to obtain employment as a musician. If she plays the trombone or the bassoon, she stands much less chance of obtaining a job than she would were she to play the harp, piano, or organ.

In short, women have never had the same opportunities, or in anything like the abundance that men have enjoyed, for the development of creativity in music; and that, it may be suspected, is one of the principal reasons why they have no spectacular achievements to their credit in this realm of art.

There have been a few women who have been brilliant performers on various instruments: Maddalena Lombardini, the eighteenth-century violinist; Clara Schumann, the pianist, and wife of Robert Schumann; the Venezuelan Teresa Carreño, who was not only the greatest woman pianist of the nineteenth century but also a distinguished opera singer, popular composer, and composer of her country's national anthem. Myra Hess was undoubtedly among the most distinguished pianists of our time, as was Wanda Landowska the most distinguished harpsichordist of our day. Though there have been a fair number of others, no one can tell how many brilliant women musicians there have been who never reached eminence because they never received the necessary encouragement.

With the exception of singing, the striking disparity between the number of men and the number of women who have achieved great distinction in music remains, but perhaps we now understand a little more clearly some of the possible reasons for this disparity.

Until her retirement in 1957 Nadia Boulanger was the world's most renowned teacher of composition.

Of women as painters John Ruskin said bluntly, "No woman can paint." But Angelica Kauffmann in the eighteenth century, Rosa Bonheur in the nineteenth century, Mary Cassatt in the nineteenth and twentieth centuries, and Marie Laurencin and Georgia O'Keeffe in the twentieth century belie his Olympian remark. Five women painters of distinction have been mentioned, but in every country there have been many extremely able women painters. In every national or international exhibition of painting there are usually present several paintings by women to which any man would be glad to put his name. Yet again we find a great disparity in the number of women who have attained distinction in painting as compared with the number of men who have done so. Obviously, reasons may be suggested for this disparity similar to those that were given for the differences in achievement in music. Incidentally, it should be added that Ruskin magnanimously retracted his opinion after he had seen the work of Elizabeth Butler, whose battle pieces, he considered, were as good as those being painted by her male contemporaries.

In sculpture, though the name of Malvina Hoffman springs to mind, there have been even fewer women of distinction than there have been in painting.

In literature, women during the last century and a half have achieved a quality that puts a number of them in the very first rank with the best of men. Fanny Burney, Jane Austen, Charlotte Brontë, and George Eliot are, by general consent, considered supreme among English women novelists. Mary Webb is by many considered to belong with these four, and most people would so class Virginia Woolf. Not many are likely to question the judgment that there have been few journalistic writers in any day who have been as good as Rebecca West.

In the United States such women novelists as Edith Wharton, Willa Cather, and Pearl Buck, the latter a Nobel Prize winner, have achieved great distinction. In Scandinavia Sigrid Undset and Selma Lagerlöf have both been awarded Nobel Prizes for their outstanding work as novelists. In Italy Grazia Deledda received the Nobel Prize as a novelist, and in Chile Gabriela Mistral received the Nobel Prize for poetry. And, of course, there is Sappho, and there is Emily Dickinson among poets.

Ever since women were first allowed upon the stage in the seventeenth century, there has been an unbroken succession of actresses of genius. From Mary Betterton, Anne Bracegirdle, and Nance Oldfield in the seventeenth and eighteenth centuries, to Rachel, Sarah Bernhardt, Duse, and Ellen Terry in more recent times, women have excelled as actresses. Here, indeed, is a field of accomplishment in which they have received every encouragement, and in which they have done surpassingly well. Possibly there is an obvious moral to be drawn.

In science, a field demanding all the qualities that have traditionally been regarded as supremely those of the male, women have been coming to the fore. We have already noted that in physics and chemistry we have the double Nobel Prize winner Marie Curie; in physics Marie Curie's daughter Irène Curie-Joliot, also a Nobel Prize winner. Another Nobel Prize winner in physics is Marie Goeppert-Mayer; in chemistry, Dorothy Hodgkin, and in physiology and medicine the Nobel Prize winner Gerty Cori. We have also previously noted that the highest scientific academies are now beginning to open their doors to women, and the English Royal Society, admission to which constitutes the highest scientific honor it is in the power of the English scientific world to bestow, already has a good sprinkling of women among its Fellows. This is also true of the National Academy of Sciences in the United States. Increasingly large numbers of women are entering the various branches of science with a view to pursuing scientific research as a career.

In my own field, anthropology, some of the most original and pathbreaking work has been done by women, and among the outstanding names in the field of anthropology that of the late Ruth Benedict, author of the classic *Patterns of Culture*, and of the dynamic

Margaret Mead will always occupy an honored place with the greatest of any time.

In the field of psychiatry, of interpersonal relations, and psychoanalysis, much highly original and important work has been done by women. I mention some names that come to mind: Theresa Benedek, Charlotte Bühler, Helene Deutsch, Anna Freud, Frieda Fromm-Reichmann, Karen Horney, Melanie Klein, Clara Thompson, and Phyllis Greenacre.

In the field of social work the outstanding name is that of Jane Addams; indeed, the whole modern social-work movement from its inception to the present day has been almost wholly a development brought about by women; and so have the kindergarten and nursery school movements.

It is not, we may suspect, by chance that when women enter the field of medicine they tend to favor such specialties as pediatrics, psychiatry, obstetrics, and anesthesia, and do best in these fields. There are, of course, many excellent women doctors in the other branches of medicine; but women do not enter these as frequently as the others mentioned, not because of the predominantly masculine grip on surgery, orthopedics, urology, otolaryngology, and the like, but because it would seem, women physicians are happier when they can give the support of their personalities, their sympathy and understanding, as well as their wisdom and skill, to their patients. The technical accomplishment of a cure or a surgical procedure does not constitute their greatest reward, as seems to be the case with the male. The male is interested in the performance of a task, in the solving of a problem; the female is concerned with its human meaning and with ministering to the need in terms of that meaning. The female doctor knows what the male doctor so seldom remembers: The care of the patient begins with caring for the patient.

It took a woman to do what no man had done before, for it was Florence Nightingale who introduced humanity into the handling and nursing of wounded soldiers. Following her arrival in the Crimea, an army major wrote, in scorn of women's knowledge of hospital work, that the first thing she had done was to order two hundred scrubbing brushes. But in spite of the hostility and the little encouragement, she initiated the organization of the first war hospital at the battlefront; and, indeed, it was she who succeeded in contributing most to making the nursing profession what it is today. It surely could have been predicted that this was one profession that women would make their own. In the United States Clara Barton played a similar role, and in addition organized the American Red Cross, being also responsible for securing the important amendment providing Red Cross relief in catastrophes other than war.

Inventions by women have never been more than 2 percent of the total accepted in any one year at the United States Patent Office. I do not know what the proportion may be for other countries, but I doubt whether there are any in which it exceeds that of the United States. As for the typical masculine comment that women have contributed not a single invention to ease their lives in the kitchen, the answer may be that women have been so busy using, among other things, the gadgets invented by men that they have had no time left over for inventing anything. Lilian Gilbreth has pointed out that "men often have good ideas about housework chiefly because they don't like it much. The engineers sometimes say that they are careful to observe the laziest person in the plant. He is the one who thinks up the short cuts." In any event, as more than one housewife has remarked, the most useful domestic gadget ever invented is a husband.

The law and the ministry have made little appeal to

women, and most churches actively discouraged them by refusing them ordination. Professions such as engineering and architecture have attracted a fair modicum of women. Of the more than 300 Federal judges in the United States in 1973, five were women. Altogether, in the various courts of the country, about 150 women held important judicial posts.

Many names of women could be cited who have done distinguished work in almost every branch of human endeavor. It is not, however, my purpose to attempt to make out a case for women as creative workers, even if it could be done, on a numerical basis. That would be silly. My purpose is to state the facts and to show by means of them that some women have achieved great distinction in every one of the fields in which they are usually so unfavorably compared with men.

In almost all the occupations mentioned, women have formed a very small proportion of the total number of persons engaged in them; hence, on a numerical basis alone, one would not expect women to excel as often as men. The important fact is that in spite of the great discrepancies in the numbers engaged, some women *do* excel. Therefore the probabilities are high that it is not a biological incapacity that is responsible for woman's excelling less frequently than man. Quite obviously there is nothing on the X-chromosomes of females which debars them from attaining great distinction in any branch of human endeavor.

But how can we say this, someone is bound to ask, since there are innumerable fields in which women have not attained great distinction? Undoubtedly this is true, but one can be reasonably safe in saying that such fields are the ones in which women have not been engaged in as large numbers as men, and most certainly not for a long period. Writing on this subject some eighty years ago, the great English humanist J. M. Robertson settled the argument with the following *responsum ad homi-nem:* No Englishman has yet written a great symphony or a great opera, and no American has yet written a great symphony, great opera, or great tragedy: Is it then reasonable to suppose that no Englishman or American is genetically capable of doing so? I leave the question to be answered by those who may feel they are competent to say whether or not any Englishman or American has done so. If adequate opportunity and stimulus are provided, great works will be created.

Have women ever been provided with such opportunities and encouragements over an adequate stretch of time?

At the time when the male is preparing for that period in his life when his creativeness is likely to be at its highest, the female is turning in a totally different direction: toward marriage and the rearing of children. During the years spent in childbearing and child rearing, not to mention the enervating domestic chores that family life entails for so many women, whatever other creative abilities she may have had tend to fall into desuetude, to become dull and atrophied. The vitality necessary for creative work becomes seriously depleted and impaired. If the male were required to do all that the average woman has always been expected to do, how much would he achieve? Most males consider it a calamity when they are called upon to perform for a few days the domestic chores with which their wives deal virtually every moment of the day, year in and year out.

A commentary on many men's understanding of women's work is provided by a communication received by Dr. Alice Chenoweth which she quotes in an article in the *Journal of the American Medical Association*: [5]

[5] 30 Jan. 1960.

Some years ago I was asked to answer a letter addressed to the "Health Department" from a mountain man. It read, in part, as follows: "Dear Sir: I am writing to ask your advice. I want some personal advice and not just some little papers or pamphlets." He went on to say that when his wife had given birth to their first and second children she had got up in a day or two and begun helping him in the fields. Then he related what happened to her in each successive pregnancy— her third, fourth, and fifth; her sixth ended in a miscarriage, By the end of the first page she had had nine pregnancies. In her tenth she had a convulsion, then followed her eleventh, twelfth, and thirteenth. And now she was pregnant for the fourteenth time. She didn't want to do anything except lie around all the time. He didn't know whether she was getting lazy or not. He had heard when women had grown children they liked to sit down and let their children wait on them. The letter ended with the question, "Can it be that my faithful wife don't want to help me anymore?"

A woman usually enters upon an occupation with a somewhat different attitude from that which characterizes the man. To a woman her occupation outside the home is important but secondary; to a man his job is of primary importance. And this constitutes yet another reason why women should not be expected to excel as men do. Men make their occupations whole-time jobs; their jobs take possession of them, and much of their time is spent in "talking shop." Women, on the other hand, rarely become possessed by any other job than that of marriage. Women do not have the capacity for dissociation that men display. Women think of marriage, home, and family as integral parts of their entire lives. Men are able to dissociate the family from their work and lead two separate existences, employing much greater concentration upon their work—because it is demanded of them—than upon their families. A woman's life is first and foremost bound up with that of her family, with her husband, her children; or if she hasn't a family of her own yet, with the hope and expectation of one.

Consider a typical situation in the professional field. The profession of medicine, for example, will bring the point out, as it were, in high relief. In medicine today, it is more likely than not that a woman will marry, and she is more likely than not to continue her career. It is, however, less than likely that she will have children, or that, having them, she will continue a full-time profession. This is the dilemma with which women in most professions are to a greater or lesser extent faced. The male, however, with his uncanny faculty for separating his mind from his heart, his reason from his emotions, his work from his home, is seldom confronted with such a dilemma. For him work and home are two utterly different worlds, so that when he comes home it is, in large measure, to a totally dissimilar way of life, with new terms and symbols and relationships. The working male doesn't have the same kind of problem that the working female has. He is able to devote all of himself to his work when he is at it, *because traditionally the male stakes his whole career upon his performance*; a woman rarely does.

For the most part women are busy creatively living the life that men can only paint or write about. Because women live creatively, they rarely experience the need to depict or write about that which to them is a primary experience and which men know only at second remove. Women create naturally—men create artificially.

Great gifts in a woman's mind and character, great achievements made by women, do not usually take the form that brings recognition and fame. Her medium is humanity, and her materials are human beings. Her greatest works remain unsigned, and fame and recognition are bestowed upon the work and not upon the artist.

In a stirring address delivered at the tenth National Woman's Rights Convention, at the Cooper Institute, in New York on 10 May 1860, Mrs. Elizabeth Cady Stanton stated the case beautifully:

If in marriage either party claims the right to stand supreme, to woman, the mother of the race, belongs the scepter and the crown. Her life is one long sacrifice for man. You tell us that among womankind there is no Moses, Christ or Paul—no Michael Angelo, Beethoven, Shakespeare—no Columbus or Galileo—no Locke or Bacon. Behold those mighty minds so grand, so comprehensive—they themselves are *our* great works! Into you, O sons of earth, goes all of us that is immortal. In you center our very life, our hopes, our intensest love. For you we gladly pour out our heart's blood and die, knowing that from our suffering comes forth a new and more glorious resurrection of thought and life.

But in the masculine-dominated world creativity in women can hardly be allowed a place. This is well illustrated by the story of the scholar who insisted that Shakespeare's plays had been written by Queen Elizabeth. The Scots minister Dr. Hugh Black challenged him. "Surely," he scoffed, "you don't believe a woman could have composed such masterpieces." "You miss my point entirely," replied the scholar. "It is my contention that Queen Elizabeth was a man."

The women who create artificially are largely the women who have been deprived of the natural creativeness of motherhood. Let the reader make a survey of the creative women of history and ask himself how many have been mothers. It is of great interest to note that many women become artificially creative after their children have grown up.

Now that women are beginning to emerge from the period of subjection, they are beginning to take an active part in the creation of those things that they formerly had no opportunity to create and that were considered the sole prerogative of men.

The world of men is highly competitive, and women traditionally simply haven't been competitors. For millennia they have not been allowed to compete with men. A woman's place was in the home, and women have from the earliest times been encouraged to look to the home and children as the fullest possible expression of their lives. If they were employed in any way, they usually regarded their employment as secondary to the most important business in life, that of having a family. Whereas men have concentrated most of their energies upon their work, most women have distributed their energies in the service of men. Men have never suffered from housemaid's knee. If men have been able to achieve as much as they have, not a little of their achievement has been due to the support that their women have given them—to the very home that the male is so effectively able to dissociate from his work! Support is another word for "love," and love is woman's métier. Woman's concentration is on love first and only secondarily upon work, profession, "achievement," and competition.

The explanation of the disparity in "achievement" of men and women is that women have simply not been as interested in the kind of achievement upon which men place so high a premium. Hence, even if from the very beginning men and women had enjoyed full and complete equality, there would still have been a vastly larger number of men than women in almost all fields of accomplishment. Because of this difference of interest, which is biologically grounded, I believe that there will always be a more or less great disparity in these types of creativity between men and women. I am not saying that women could not do as well as men if they could be interested in doing what men do, for I think they probably could; all that I am saying is that women, because they are women, are more interested in human relationships, in which they can creatively love and be loved. As long as this remains the true genius of women, the world will be safe for humanity. On the day when women begin to outstrip men in the fields of worldly achievement, the human race will have to take its temperature. But I do not think that day will ever come, *not* because women aren't as intelligent or as well endowed with genius as men, but because women will increasingly tend to realize their intelligence and their genius in the most important of all areas for human beings—human relationships.

11.

The Genius of Woman
as the Genius
of Humanity

WOMAN IS THE CREATOR and fosterer of life; man has been the mechanizer and destroyer of life. The fact that men cannot have babies and suckle them, nor remain in association with their children as closely as the mother, has an enormous effect upon their subsequent psychological development. Altogether apart from the psychological influences due to sexual physiological differences, one can safely say that the mother-child relationship confers benefits upon the mother that are wanting between father and child. The maternalizing influences of being a mother have, from the very beginning of the human species, made the female the more humane of the sexes. The love of a mother for her child is the basic patent and model for all human relationships. Indeed, to the degree to which men approximate in their relationships with their fellow men the love of the mother for her child, to that extent do they move more closely toward the attainment of genuine humanity. The mother-child relationship is an inter-dependent one. The interstimulation between mother and child is something the father misses, and he suffers from the want of it. In short, the female in the mother-child relationship has the advantage of having to be more considerate, more self-sacrificing, more coopera-tive, and more altruistic than usually falls to the lot of the male.

The female thus acquires, in addition to whatever natural biological advantages she starts with, a compe-tence in social understanding which is usually denied the male. The sensitive relationships that exist between mother and child belong to a unique order of humanity, an order in which the male may participate as a child, but from which he increasingly departs as he leaves childhood behind. Not so the female, whose practice in the art of human relations continues throughout life; and this is one of the additional reasons that enable women to perceive the nuances and pick up the sub-liminal signs in human behavior which men usually fail to perceive. Because women have had to be unselfish, forbearing, self-sacrificing, and maternal, they possess a deeper understanding than men of what it means to be human. Women live the whole spectrum of life; they do not think in terms of achromatic black and white, Yes and No, or in terms of the all-or-none principle, as men are inclined to do. Women don't settle matters of life and death by saying, "Put him up against a wall and shoot him." They are inclined to say, rather, "Give him another chance." Women are more ready to make adjust-ments, to consider the alternative possibilities, and to see the other colors and gradations in the range between black and white.

By comparison with the deep involvement of women in living, men appear to be only superficially engaged.

Compare the love of a male for a female with the love of the female for the male. It is the difference between a rivulet and a great deep ocean. In Byron's words:

> *Man's love is of man's life a thing apart,*
> *'Tis woman's whole existence.*

Women love the human race; men behave as if they were, on the whole, hostile to it. Men act as if they haven't been adequately loved, as if they had been rejected, frustrated, and rendered hostile. Becoming aggressive, they say that aggressiveness is natural, and that women are inferior because they tend to be gentle and unaggressive! But it is precisely in the capacity to love, in their cooperativeness rather than aggressiveness, that the superiority of women to men is demonstrated; for whether it be natural to be loving and cooperative or not, as far as the human species is concerned, its evolutionary destiny, its very survival, are more closely tied to the capacity for love and cooperation than to anything else.

It is in this, of course, that women can realize their power for good in the world, and make their greatest gains. *It is the function of women to teach men how to be human.* Women must not permit themselves to be deflected from their function by those who tell them that their place is in the home, in subservient relation to man. It is, indeed, in the home that the foundations of the kind of world in which we live are laid, and in this sense it will always remain true that the hand that rocks the cradle is the hand that rules the world. And it is in this sense that women must assume the task of making men who will know how to participate in the process of making a world fit for human beings to live in. The greatest single step forward in this direction will be made when women consciously assume the task of teaching their children to be, like themselves, loving and cooperative.

Having been made to feel inferior to men all their lives, it seems only "natural" to expect many women to react to the feeling of inferiority, which the male-dominated world has produced in them, with behavior calculated to demonstrate that they are as "good" as men. By such behavior women do themselves and the world a disservice. Women do not have to, and should not, compete with men. They should not compete with anyone, any more than men should. Women and men should cooperate. That is what they were intended to do by nature, and that is what it is their nature to do. The function of women is not to outdo men but to do for men what women alone are capable of doing; namely, to prepare them as children for the job of being good human beings. Men must fully and sympathetically understand that it is not their job that is the most important, but that it is the job of the woman, the mother—the most significant job in the world. Men must understand that if anyone is competitively handicapped in this connection, it is not the female but the male. But why speak of handicaps? Only to clarify them. Men have made women feel that childbearing and child rearing are handicaps that prevent women from competing with men. The most important jobs in the world handicaps! The poor male. And yet this piece of nonsense, wrongheaded and stupid and awful as it is, has caused some women, particularly in our own time, to react with an overweening desire to compete with men in their own fields, on their own ground, in order to "show 'em." How wrongheaded both attitudes are! Neither man nor woman should ever work in order to compete.

A thorough understanding of the differences between

male and female, while leading to a promotion of the female, also leads to a promotion—not a demotion—of the male; for men, through better understanding, will be enabled to realize their potentialities quite as fully as women. This is an area in which both men and women can work together most cooperatively and creatively, in getting to understand each other better, in learning to think jointly, and in contributing to each other's happier development.

As the distinguished American naturalist, William Emerson Ritter (1856–1944) wrote in his last book, *Darwin and the Golden Rule,*

It appears to me certain that a major factor in hastening the socialization of the male will be his getting a deeper insight than he seems ever to have had into the real nature of the female in relation to the whole sexual, domestic, communal and political complex.[1]

Both men and women must clearly understand the significance of women's performing the role of mothers, of women's bearing, giving birth to, and being largely responsible for caring for and molding the development of the child. This, we now know, is the most important of all the tasks that any human being can perform for another. Indeed, the findings of contemporary scientific investigations in this area have shown that no less than the future of mankind depends upon the manner in which the task is carried out. By virtue of the female's being biologically equipped to bear and nurse children, she stands in the most fundamental relationship it is possible for one human being to stand in in relation to another; namely, as the support and sustainer without whom the child could not survive during its first nine months in the womb, and thereafter in only a crippled

[1] New York: Storm Publishers, 1954, p. 203.

sort of way unless a person can be found who will perform the functions of a mother. The function of the mother is to love her child. That statement contains all that it would be necessary to say on the subject were it not that a large number of persons in our culture do not understand the meaning of love.

It is here that a note of caution must be sounded. The Women's Liberation Movement has done magnificent work, but as in all movements there are some extremists in it who argue that those who plead the need of motherhood, who emphasize the importance of mothering in the first few years of the child, are nothing but male chauvinist pigs who are engaged in a conspiracy to perpetuate the servitude of the female. Some women in the movement are apparently desperately in need of enemies, for even in the face of the abundant evidence [2] they continue to maintain that a good day care center can do just as well as a mother. *Some* mothers, no doubt, and even better. But for the genuinely loving mother there can be no substitute, whether she be biological or surrogate. When a baby is born, a mother is born too. It is a false view of liberation to believe that motherhood is a role from which women should be liberated. Liberated from what to what? From the oppressions, discriminations, and injustices from which they have suffered, most certainly. But if women ever come to believe that they will be freed from the necessity of being mothers to their children, and that being a mother is somehow inferior to being a career

[2] It is fully dealt with in Ashley Montagu, *The Direction of Human Development* (New York: Hawthorn Books, 1970). Also in Ashley Montagu, *On Being Human* (New York: Hawthorn Books, 1967). See also John Bowlby, *Attachment and Loss,* vol. 1, *Attachment* (New York: Basic Books, 1969). Harry F. Harlow and M. K. Harlow, "Learning to Love," *American Scientist,* 54, 1966, 244–272; H. F. Harlow, "Primary Affectional Patterns in Primates," *American Journal of Orthopsychiatry,* 30, 1960, 676–684.

woman, they will have betrayed themselves, and revealed how profoundly they have been brainwashed into accepting the mythology that males have imposed upon them. For the truth is that being a mother is the most important career anyone can be called upon to follow.

Women can and should enter any occupation or profession they choose. But when they become mothers they must realize that they have entered the most important of all the occupations and professions combined, for what can be more important than the making of a loving human being? The demeaning references made by some women liberationists to children or else their complete disregard of them indicates how dangerous some of these female chauvinists may be. The claims of children are not incompatible with the rights of women, and any attempt to secure such rights at the cost of those of children imperils all our rights. To see the child as an object rather than as a person is to reduplicate the offense that men have for so long committed against women. Women have a right to refuse to have children, but if they do have them they cannot abdicate their role in shaping their future. When Dr. Spock says "I myself would say it is much more creative to rear and shape the personality of a fine, live child than it is to work in an office or even to carve a statue," women's liberationists may jeer him, as they did at their Political Caucus meeting in Washington in July, 1971, but who else would disagree?

As Ian Suttie put it in his magnificent book, *The Origins of Love and Hate*, "Any social factors therefore which stunt the character-development of women, contract her interests or lower her prestige with her children will interfere with her function of promoting the maturation of her children and their independence of herself." [3] And as Suttie goes on to show, disturbances in the maternal capacity to love are the root cause of mental illness.

What is love? "Fool!" exclaimed Sir Philip Sidney, "look in thy heart, and write." But were any scientist to do so, his colleagues would almost certainly object. So let me, in plain English, and basing my answer on the interpretation of scientific findings, define love as the state of responsiveness to others during which one conveys to them the feeling that one is tenderly interested in them, that one will support them and minister to their needs. To be tenderly regardful and wholeheartedly involved in the needs of another is love. It means behavior calculated to confer survival benefits upon the other in a creatively enlarging manner. Not merely to enable them to live longer, but to live more fully realized than they would otherwise be. It means to communicate to the other your profound involvement in their welfare, such that they can depend upon your being there to minister to their needs, to give them all the supports, sustenances, and stimulations they require for their growth and development as warm, loving human beings. It means to communicate to them that you will never commit the supreme treason of letting them down when they most stand in need of you, but that you will be there whenever they have need of your answering to their need. That is love.[4] And that is what women, when they are not confused and rendered overanxious or turned into social workers in their own homes, have given or attempted to give their children. Where they have successfully been able to give such love to their children, the personality of the adult shows its effects, even though many other elements have

[3] Baltimore: Penguin Books, 1960, p. 207.
[4] For a full development of this subject see Ashley Montagu, *The Direction of Human Development*.

entered into the making of that personality. Such a person will himself be capable of entering into meaningful relationships, of loving others, and of cooperating with them.

Unfortunately, in many cultures, including our own, the natural capacity of women to love their children is made to express itself in a social matrix that often distorts and nullifies it, with resulting serious consequences to the development of the personality of the child and the person into which he will grow.

The most important thing in the world for a developing human being to enjoy is love. Fathers are parents too, and their love for their children is important; but when everything has been said and done the love of the father does not compare in fundamental importance with the love of the mother for her child. Indeed, so long as the occupational roles of the parents in our society remain what they are, no one can ever take the place of the mother. (The mother does not necessarily have to be the biological mother so long as the mother surrogate behaves as a mother to the child.)

If men continue to force their views upon women of how a family, a society, and a world should be run, and if women continue to act as the executors of men's will, the world will remain in that unhappy plight in which it finds itself at the present time; but together men and women can remold it nearer the heart's desire by recognizing that the best way to make loving, cooperative, harmonic, nonhostile human beings is by being loving, cooperative, harmonic, and nonhostile toward children. Men can help women make better men, as well as better women, by permitting women to realize their potentialities for being human to the fullest. The most satisfactory way in which men can serve themselves in this connection is by encouraging women to realize their potentialities for loving their children. The best way of remaking the world is not by changing the world but by changing the people who make the world the kind of place it is, by making human beings out of people. Unfortunately we have changed the environment more rapidly and more substantially than we have changed ourselves. Each of us must ask ourselves what we are doing that is really relevant to the world in which we are living.

Almost everyone will agree that there have been more geniuses for being human among women than there have been among men. The true genius of women is the genius for being human. In our materialistic age, because we have placed far less value upon the qualities for being human than we have upon those for accomplishment in the arts, sciences, and technologies, our values have become confused, undeveloped, and we have almost forgotten what the true ones are. Surely the most valuable quality in any human being is his capacity for being loving and cooperative. We have been placing our emphases on the wrong values, and it is time we recognized what every man and every woman, at the very least subconsciously, knows—the value of being loving and the value of those who can teach this better than anyone else.

I hope I shall not be taken for an anti-intellectual when I say that intellect without humanity, without love, is not good enough, and that what the world is suffering from at the present time is not so much an overabundance of intellect as an insufficiency of humanity. Consider men like Karl Marx, Lenin, Stalin, and Hitler, as well as a number of others, at the moment still "respectable," whom I must forbear to mention. They are the extreme cases. What these men have lacked is quite obviously the capacity to love. What they have possessed in so eminent a degree has been the capacity to hate and to be unforgiving. It is not for nothing that the Soviets attempted to abolish the family and masculinize women, while the Nazis made informers of children against their parents and put the state so much before the family that it became a behemoth that well nigh destroyed everyone who was victimized by it.

What the world stands so much in need of at the present time, and what it will continue to need if it is to endure and grow in happiness, is more of the maternal spirit and less of the masculine. We need more givers of life and fewer takers of it. We need more persons who will love and less who will hate, and we need to understand how to teach them to do so; for if we do not try to understand we shall continue to flounder in the morass of misunderstanding that frustrated love creates. The tendencies to love with which the infant is born are frustrated, and frustrated love results in hostility. Hatred is love frustrated. That is what too many men suffer from, and what an insufficient number of women recognize—at least too many women behave as if they fail to recognize it. What most women have learned to recognize is that the much-bruited superiority of the male isn't all that men, so loudly advertising their own wares, have claimed it to be. The male seems to be neither so steady nor so wise as women were taught to believe. But on this subject there appears to be a conspiracy of silence. Perhaps women feel that men ought to be maintained in the illusion of their superiority because it might not be good for them or for the world to learn the truth. In that sense this book might have been entitled "What Every Woman Knows." But one can't be sure that every woman knows it. What one can be sure of is that many women don't appear to know it, and even that there are many women who are horrified at the thought that anyone can possibly entertain the idea that women are anything but inferior to men. And there is the hostility of women toward their own sex, reflected in Lady Wortley Montagu's remark, "It goes far to reconcile me to being a woman, that I reflect that I am thus in no danger of marrying one." This sort of thinking does no one any good. The world is in a mess. Men, without any assistance from women, have created the mess, not because they have been failed by women but because men have never really given women a chance to serve them as they are best equipped to do—by teaching men how to love their fellow men.

Women must cease supporting men for the wrong reasons in the wrong sort of way and thus cease enabling men to marry them for the wrong reasons, too. "That's what a man wants in a wife, mostly," says Mrs. Poyser, in *Adam Bede*, "he wants to make sure o' one fool as 'ull tell him he's wise." But women, as James Stephens wrote, are wiser than men because they know less and understand more. Serving as natural mirrors, they have helped men reflect to twice their natural size. It is time that men learned the truth, and perhaps they are likely to take it more gracefully from another male than from their unacknowledged betters. It is equally important that women learn the truth too, for it is to them that the most important part, the more fundamental part, of the task of remaking the world will fall, for the world will be remade only by helping human beings to realize themselves more fully in terms of what their mothers have to give them. Without adequate mothers life becomes intolerable, and Mother Earth becomes a battlefield upon which fathers participate in the slaying of their young and are themselves diminished.

Though men have had a long tenure in mismanaging the affairs of the world, it is time that women realize that men will continue to run the world for some time yet, and that women can best assist them to run it more intelligently and more humanely by teaching them, when young, what humanity means. Thus men will not feel that they are being demoted but rather that their potentialities for good are greatly increased. What is more important, instead of feeling hostile toward women they will for the first time learn to appreciate them at their proper worth. An old Spanish proverb says that a good wife is the workmanship of a good husband. Perhaps. But of one thing we can be certain: A good husband is the workmanship of a good mother. The best of all ways in which men can help themselves is to help women realize themselves. In this way both sexes will come for the first time fully into their own, and mankind may then look forward to a happier history than it has thus far enjoyed.

The genius of woman is the genius of humanity, and humanity is the supreme form of intelligence. Mankind must learn to understand that all other forms of intelligence must be secondary to the developed *humane* intelligence, for any form of intelligence that is not primarily implanted into a matrix of humane feeling and understanding is the most dangerous thing in the world. The clever can never be too clever when they are governed by the desire and the ability to think of the welfare of others—even before they think of their own—for so to think and conduct oneself is to serve oneself better than one may in any other manner.

It is that kind of intelligence that the world stands most in need of at the present time. It is that kind of intelligence that the world will always stand most in need of. It is that kind of intelligence with which women are so abundantly endowed. It is that kind of intelligence that it is their destiny to teach the world.

12.

Mutual Aid

IN THIS BOOK I have had to deal with certain myths about women, myths that have grown hoary with the ages, and I have had to set out the facts. The facts, for the most part, completely controvert the myths, and the facts prove that, on the whole, the advantages are on the side of the female. This conclusion alone will be sufficient to elicit the sympathetic interest of most women and bring them rallying, even more devotedly than ever, to the sides of their males—which is precisely as it should be. Men need women even more than women need men. This is not to say that women don't need men; they do—very much—but not as basically, pressingly, as men need women; for just as a child needs the love of a mother if it is to develop healthily, so a man needs the love of a woman to maintain him in good mental and physical health. For his complete and adequate functioning he is more *dependent* upon such love than a woman is. In such a fundamental human situation women will not dream of considering themselves as anything but helpmeets to men. One can only wish that men would more profoundly understand what the medieval English poet Geoffrey Chaucer so well expressed almost six hundred years ago:

> For this ye know well, tho' I wouldin lie,
> In women is all truth and steadfastness;
> For in good faith, I never of them sie
> But much worship, bounty, and gentleness,
> Right coming, fair, and full of meekéness;
> Good, and glad, and lowly, I you ensure,
> Is this goodly and angelic creature.
>
> And if it hap a man be in disease,
> She doth her business and her full pain,
> With all her might him to comfort and to please,
> If fro his disease him she might restrain:
> In word ne deed, I wis, she woll not faine;
> With all her might she doth her business
> To bringen him out of his heaviness.
>
> Lo, here what gentleness these women have
> If we could know it for our rudéness!
> How busy they be us to keep and save
> Both in hele and also in sicknèss,
> And always right sorry for our distress!
> In evéry manere thus show they ruth,
> That in them is all goodness and all truth.

"For this ye know well . . ." Of course we do. But why in the name of goodness we men have done so little about this knowledge, and left it till so late, perhaps constitutes a commentary on our lack of understanding of ourselves. We have been scared and we have been confused, and we have had to live within the framework of the male-dominated society into which we have been born. Something of the truth of Chaucer's words every man knows—which is a good point of departure on the rewarding journey of learning to know more—why

Chaucer wrote a *Legend of Good Women* but no *Legend of Good Men.* Men can help women and women can help men. Men *should* help women—women will help men, anyway. The sexes are interdependent in a manner so biologically fundamental, their functions are so basically reciprocal, and they are so delicately related to each other that any failure in adjustment between them is likely to have serious personal and social group consequences. Perhaps it need not be emphasized that such lack of adjustment has been characteristic of the greater part of mankind for an extremely long time, and that the consequences have been serious. Just as the lack of adjustment between mother and infant may do irreparable harm to the mental health of the infant, so the lack of adjustment between the sexes has done damage to men and women and their children, and to the societies they constitute. Men cannot keep one-half the human race in subjection and expect to escape the havoc they thus cause in themselves.

The tragedy is that modern men are caught in the web of a tradition they never made—a tradition that came to them as part of their social heredity but that they most often mistake as being part of the biological order of things. But if men were conditioned in the truth, if they were afforded opportunities for studying and learning the facts, and if they were brought up in a society that hung question marks on hoary traditions and on ideas that were taken for granted, they might successfully disentangle themselves from the web of false traditional beliefs about women.

It is, however, not only a matter of disentangling oneself from the entanglements of the old and fallacious ideas and practices but a question also of adjusting oneself to a new conception of the relations between the sexes. In these tasks women and men will have to work together; they will *need* to work together, to cooperate; and by doing so they can free each other from the shackles that have bound them for so long. By working together in harmony, men and women will confer the greatest benefits upon each other and upon the whole of humanity.

These are nice sentiments; but now let us proceed to a discussion of the rationale, the scientific basis for such ideas, so that the reader may judge for himself how well founded such recommendations are.

First I should like the reader to understand something of the basic meaning of social relationships; this done, we may then proceed to the discussion of the practical significance of the facts for the improvement of the relations between the sexes.

It is a convenient academic device to start with the simplest types of organisms in order to show students as simply as possible the main facts about an organism's functioning. I shall follow this procedure here. Remember, we are interested in the nature of social relationships.

If, under natural conditions, we observe a simple one-celled organism like the ameba, we shall generally find it in association with other amebae. Now, if we look at a number of amebae long enough under a microscope we shall find that when the single ameba has reached a certain size it begins to reduplicate itself, that is, to reproduce. By studying the process of reproduction carefully, you will find (I shall omit a number of unnecessary details here) that the nucleus of the ameba divides into two, and that the new nucleus flows into the protoplasm to the side of the maternal nucleus. There it remains within the protoplasm while certain other changes are going on, still quite within the same maternal cell membrane. Any changes induced in the protoplasm will mutually be responded to by both the maternal cell and the daughter cell that is coming into being.[1] Whatever affects the one affects the other. There is a complete exchange of physiologically necessary substance between the maternal and daughter cells while they are still within the same cell membrane. There is complete interdependent relationship; one is dependent upon the other.

Every living thing comes into being originally in this fundamentally similar interdependent manner. It is in the process of origin of one living thing from another, in the biologic relation of interdependency which the reproductive process constitutes, that the fundamental meaning of social relationships, of social life, is to be sought and understood. It is, indeed, in the pattern of interdependency that has been described for the single-celled organism that the significance of social relationships in the most complex of many-celled organisms is to be understood, for interdependency, no matter how complex the organism or how simple, is the basic pattern of the social state. Indeed, the earliest source of social drives may be perceived as an outgrowth of the original biologic interdependent relationship between genitor cell and offspring cell in the process of reproduction. Physical relatedness evolves to a much higher order of psychological complexity, but whatever the origin of relatedness, interdependency is the social condition that characterizes all living organisms, that is, responsiveness between organisms, or interactive behavior.

The social state is the process of interaction between organisms during which they confer survival benefits upon one another. In other words, social relationships

---

[1] It should be explained that it is the custom to refer to the genitor cell as the maternal cell, and the offspring cell as the daughter cell. Some biologists prefer to speak of both cells as sister cells. Whichever terminology one adopts depends upon the school to which one belongs. It does not make the least difference which terminology one uses so long as one uses it consistently.

are an extension and amplification of the physiologic relations obtaining between maternal organism and offspring. The suggestion is that apart from the very nature of protoplasm itself, which is cohesive, both maternal organism and offspring in the process of reproduction undergo an intensification of their physiologically cohesive or interdependent energies, with the result that the offspring experience strong impulses of attraction that cause them to remain in association with the organism or organisms of the same kind; while the maternal organism, as a consequence of the reproductive process, finds that her own tendencies for social aggregation are intensified and focused upon the needs of her offspring.

With the possible exception of certain lower forms, throughout the whole kingdom of life organisms are found in association—indeed, all organisms are social. Excluding, possibly, certain insects, if one ever finds a solitary animal in nature it is either only temporarily dissociated from its social group or something else is wrong. In fact, when any living creature begins to isolate itself from the group, and tends to remain isolated, one can be certain that something is awry, or else that such behavior is actually conferring survival benefits upon the group. In short, social interaction and responsiveness is a well-nigh universal concomitant of life. Cooperation, not conflict, is the law of life.

Several years ago, as reported by Professor Chauncey D. Leake, a group of distinguished American scientists formulated the following principle: "The probability of survival of a relationship between individual humans increases with the extent to which that relationship is mutually satisfying." This is, of course, a special case of the more general principle: "The probability of survival of individual or groups of living things increases with the degree with which they harmoniously adjust themselves to each other and to their environment."

These principles apply to all human relationships without exception, and with particular force to the male-female, husband-wife relationships.

When we examine the manner in which these principles actually work in all groups, we find that the benefits conferred upon those mutually participating are striking. In addition to the great psychological benefits conferred, it has been found that in human beings every physical system of the body is benefited as well. Psychosomatic medicine is a living testimony to that truth. It has been found in recent years that children do not grow properly if their socio-emotional relationships are disturbed. Dr. Ralph Fried of Cleveland published a most impressive study on the subject, and workers in Canada and elsewhere independently made the same discoveries. May it not be that the psychosocial subjection in which women have been kept for many millennia has some connection with their greater sickness rate? Response to a continuously depressing environment often takes the form of chronic or frequent illness. On the other hand, when organisms—any kind of organisms—live together under cooperative conditions they contribute to one another in such a way as to enrich what can only be described as the faculty to live.

To love thy neighbor as thyself is not only sound ethics but perfectly good biology; it is not only good text material for Sunday sermons but the best of all principles by which to live one's life. The most immediate relationships in which this principle can best be applied are those of husband and wife, parents and children. If parents would learn what is known about these matters, and apply the knowledge in their family relationships—as all of them, I am sure, would be more than willing to do if they possessed it—the greater part of the world's human problems would be solved, for it is in the home that human beings are formed, and it is human beings who mold the world according to the kingdom that is within them. We must understand that it is in the nature, *dominantly* in the nature, of human beings to be cooperative, to want to love and be loved. It is *not* in the nature of human beings to be aggressive and hostile. Aggressiveness and hostility are the responses of an organism that is frustrated, that has been thwarted in its expected satisfactions of love; such an organism turns to aggression in order to attract, to compel toward itself the love it seeks. Hostility arises when the organism feels itself both frustrated and threatened.

It is only very recently that we have learned to understand these things as scientists; men of religion, prophets, seers, poets, and philosophers have understood them for thousands of years, while the remainder of poor struggling humanity has painfully endeavored to climb the ladder of their high ideals. But it has not been given to many of them to ascend beyond its lowest rungs. The source of much of man's difficulty has lain in the fact that for the greater part of humanity the struggle for survival has been an unremittingly hard one, and in the course of it men have been forced into ways of life that hold the promise of being beneficial to themselves though they may be inimical to the interests of others. That some individuals have behaved in such a manner in all times is possible, but there is good reason to believe that such behavior on the part of most of the members of a human society is a fairly recent development in the history of man. When men first began to grow into the ways of urban civilization, not more than fifteen thousand years ago, and began to exploit their fellow men as commodities, the ability to obtain the advantages that an urban civilization could confer set a new standard of "success." Success was now no longer seen as being a good, cooperative member of one's society, but as the securing of the money and the power to increase the material comforts of life. Though spiritual success was not denied as a possibility, as something toward which one should strive, the success that received increasing attention was material success.

The progress we flatter ourselves as having made since prehistoric times has been great, but in a very real sense it has meant a progress at the cost of many of our humane values. Our progress has been concentrated upon *things*, while spiritual values and our preoccupation with the truly good life have been allowed to lag, even to fall into desuetude. It sometimes seems that for every step forward we have taken in science and technology, we have taken one backward in morality; for every step forward we have taken in material civilization, we have taken one backward in moral development. Hitler's extermination of millions of human beings, the dropping of atom bombs, government by terror, fascism, communism, war, the competitive relation of man to man—all these things and much else appear to be evidence of a very real and serious deterioration of man as a moral human being. It is not that prehistoric man lived in a Golden Age, as some thinkers have imagined—it was undoubtedly far from "golden." But of one thing we can be virtually certain: Men were far more interested in one another's welfare than men of the Western civilizations of the world seem to be today. Had this not been so, no human group could have survived to the present day.

The principal disorders of Western man today may be traced to the development of the competitive way of life in an increasingly competitive industrial world. However, it was not until the eighteenth century that it acquired a terrifying momentum that has accelerated with dizzying speed during the last two hundred years. The Industrial Revolution revolutionized the lives of the greater part of mankind; though it brought great benefits it also brought great disasters in its wake. Commerce, it has been said, through competition, is the life-blood of a nation. All things compete, said Darwin. Evolution and the progression of species come about by means of a struggle for existence, through competition, and by the selection for survival of the fittest competitors. Society, opined the sociologist Herbert Spencer, mirrors the struggle for existence which is constantly going on in a state of nature. War is natural and good, said the generals, because it delivers the only just judgment on the fitness of nations to survive. You've got to be a go-getter, says the American creed, because if you're not, someone else will go out and get what you want. You must get the highest marks, be first, be out in front, because this is a competitive world and the race is to the swift and you've got to be a football hero to make a hit with the beautiful girls even if it means breaking the leg of another player who is known to have a bad knee, or stepping on his hand and crushing it deliberately because he belongs to a minority group, or resorting to conduct that outrages every tenet of decency and sportsmanship. It's Civilization; Man's Own Show; Rugged American Individualism, you know. Well, America has made some progress, not because of competition, but in spite of competition—because people have frequently got together and done things. Competition is the striving of men *against* each other in order to attain the same goal. Greatest progress has been made when they have striven *with* each other to attain the same goal. But cooperation and competition have been sadly confused and intermixed, and the resulting disorder and its effects are nowhere better seen than in the United States, the land in which the competitive spirit is most highly developed.

America is one of the few countries in which it is possible to apply the term "aggressive" to a person in a flattering way. We like our men to be "tough"; we don't like our boys to be "sissies," because they've got to go out and "fight" for themselves. The tragedy is that many women have been trapped by this rough masculine creed into teaching their children to be competitors. Mothers will even bargain with their children for love that should be unconditional, and the birthright of every child: "Junior, if you don't eat your cereal you won't make the football team, because you won't develop the necessary muscles, and Mama won't love you." In this, and many other ways, Mother bargains with Junior for his love. Perhaps no American mother has uttered just those words, but most of us know from innumerable experiences that many mothers convey the essential meaning of such words to their children. Margaret Mead has appropriately called this bargaining type of love "conditional love." Junior must be a greater success than his father was, and, of course, Mary must do better for herself than Mama did. At the same time the children will receive an ethicoreligious training, in which they are told on the one hand that they must love their neighbors as themselves, and on the other that they must go out and compete with their neighbors. This is very confusing, and to most children—particularly adolescents—disturbing. Are adults hypocrites? Do they believe what they *say* or what they *do*? Quite rightly, children decide that adults believe what they do, not what they say. And so they go out and do likewise. In this way the vicious circle is perpetuated. The naturally cooperative organism is taught to be competitive, even though the ideals of the religion to which he may have been exposed teach cooperation, with a resultant conflict within himself which is never successfully resolved. Cooperation and competition are not mutually reconcilable drives. Either you are a cooperator or you are a competitor; if you are both, then you are in a state of disoperativeness, of confusion, unreconciled and in conflict with yourself. And this is the state in which most members of Western civilization find themselves; this is the state that is essentially identified with the masculine spirit, the masculine role in society; this is the state from which men need to be weaned.

In our culture mothers learn to reject the love of their sons, a love which the sons offer unconditionally but which mother cannot wholly accept. Unconscious, half-conscious, or conscious anxieties about incest, mother attachments, or fear of making the boy too soft cause many mothers to make the little rejections of their small sons' love which to the child constitute a very real privation and frustration. The father's participation in this process in the form either of an unconscious or of a conscious jealousy of his son's place in the affection of his wife, complicated by the little boy's jealousy of his father, adds to the boy's feeling of privation and frustration and contributes to his store of aggressiveness and hostility. Clearly, the mother-son relationship is a particularly delicate one and requires the most sympathetic and gentle understanding.

If to be tough and crude and crass and competitive is to be a man, and if to be gentle, tender, kind, considerate, and cooperative is to be a sissy, then in the name of all humanity let us have fewer men and more sissies! But why grant the confused the solace of their own confusion or fall into their confusion by using their terms? What they contemptuously refer to by the term "sissy" constitutes the qualities usually associated with the female; and no man can bear the imputation of being in any way like the "inferior" sex. But those very feminine qualities are the essential qualities of humanity—gentleness, kindness, thoughtfulness, and cooperativeness—and in so far as men have departed from these qualities they have departed from the true path of humanity. By this I do not mean to suggest anything so absurd as that it would be a good thing for humanity if men became women! I *do* mean to suggest that if little boys were helped to be gentle, kind, thoughtful, and cooperative, they would easily become so in their own masculine way. And in that endeavor, fathers as well as mothers can help. If fathers will themselves place a little less emphasis on being rough and tough, and more on being gentle, tender, and kind themselves, particularly in relation to their wives, their sons will observe, and do likewise, and humanity will be bound to make great advances in the right direction.

We have to understand that what any society considers to be the gender roles of "masculinity" and "femininity" are purely arbitrary. "Male" and "female" are terms which refer to biological sex, not to gender sex. A biological male may by gender role be feminine, and a biological female may by gender role be masculine, and each may be all the gradations in between. A survey of the societies of the world shows that the vast majority of them are organized by and around males rather than females, and that statuses and roles are subject to this male dominance. Based on the biological differences between the sexes men have erected a superstructure of expectations, obligations, rights, and duties that they call statuses and roles. These gender roles are quite arbitrary, and their determinance by men has led to every conceivable discrimination by them against women. The long entrenched dominance of the asymmetric gender roles in most societies has so solidified them that they have come to be accepted by almost everyone as expressions of the laws of nature. It is, for example, in the Western world generally believed that gender is a biologically, a genetically determined status. The fundamental error committed here is that gender is confused with sex. Sex is biologically determined, gender is for the most part learned. The evidence for this is now beyond dispute.[2]

The species traits of *Homo sapiens* are educability, plasticity, and malleability, and it is particularly important at this critical period in our social development to understand that fact, to understand what it means. What is meant is that within the limits of what is possible human beings are capable of learning anything. That whatever the biological or physiological components that enter into sexual behavior, sexual status, and sexual gender, their character, form, and expression is a function of the interaction between genetic potentials and the environments in which those potentials undergo development. What the evidence indicates is that everywhere in human societies sexual behavior, gender, and yes, even society itself, are determined not by genetic potentials, but by the action of the individual's learning experience upon those potentials. It is what society does to the genetic potentialities, and not what genetic potentialities do to society that makes human institutions. The genetic potentialities are possibilities and within the range of those possibilities culture can do virtually anything with them. In short, with the exception of the reproductive roles, sex roles and the roles of sex are what we choose to make them. And what we need to do

---

[2] For detailed discussions see Robert J. Stoller, *Sex & Gender* (New York: Science House, 1968); Ann Oakley, *Sex, Gender & Society* (New York: Harper & Row, 1972); John Money and Anke E. Ehrhardt, *Man & Woman Boy & Girl* (Baltimore: Johns Hopkins University Press, 1972); Joseph Zubin and John Money (editors), *Contemporary Sexual Behavior* (Baltimore: Johns Hopkins University Press, 1973).

is to humanize those roles by transforming them into the function of a loving relationship rather than the tyranny and exploitation of one sex by another. And this, I believe, each of us can at least approximate, if we would but make the effort.

I thoroughly agree with Carolyn Heilbrun who, in her book *Toward a Recognition of Androgyny*,[3] has pointed out the dangers of an ideal of masculinity which emphasizes the characteristics of competitiveness, aggressiveness, and defensiveness. By placing such men in positions of power, we have greatly endangered our survival and ensured such disasters as Vietnam, My Lai, and Kent State and will continue in the brutalizing environment of the man-made world.

The traits that men have called "feminine": gentleness, tenderness, lovingkindness, are not feminine traits but human traits, and they are the very traits that men need to adopt and develop if they are ever to be returned to a semblance of humanity.

The important thing for men to understand is why it is desirable to be kind and cooperative. The brief answer to that "why," which has been set out at greater length in the preceding pages and elsewhere, is that it is to the advantage of everyone to be so. To be cooperative means not only to confer survival benefits upon the cooperators but also to enlarge their capacity for living; it means the production of harmony, health, wealth, and happiness; it means to restore to human beings their ability to love and their ability to work—their mental health; and it means an end to conflict on the interpersonal plane and eventually on the international plane. Someone has defined civilization as the process of learning to be kind. That is precisely what we need to do—to become more civilized, to learn to be kind.

[3] New York: A. A. Knopf, 1973.

It is not sufficient for men to be kind to their children, which as yet they are far from being: they must be kind to their wives also, to all women. Men need to understand that the principle of cooperation, like charity, begins at home, and that the best place to begin anew with the development of their own characters and their children's is in their relationships with their wives. The husband-wife relationship is the proving ground, as well as the testing ground, of character. No less an authority than Balzac remarked that marriage was the best school for a man's character that was ever devised. For both sexes marriage should be a continuing, and the best, part of one's education for living. It should be a mutual exchange of experience and stimulation contributing to the greater creative growth and development of each, of supports and assistances, of mutual working out of problems, of sharing and preparing for the requirements of parenthood and of being human in a world at war with itself. Above all, marriage must be based on mutual respect; and in the present state of the relations of the sexes I should add that on the man's part it should be accompanied by a sense of responsibility and obligation to the woman of his choice.

Men should feel it one of the obligations of marriage to make available, as far as it lies in their power, all the assistance they can to help their wives be more effectively what they desire to be. Men must realize, more profoundly than they seem to have done so far, what it is to be a domestic slave; they must learn that a woman should not be exclusively required to be her husband's maidservant, laundress, cook, and concubine, nurse and governess to the children, spending the first quarter of a century of her married life so employed, and the next twenty-five years recovering from the effects of bringing up the children, still unrelieved of her other duties. A woman is a person in her own right who wants to be, and should be, treated as something more than the good companion who happens also to be one's domestic slave.

Men *are* altering their attitudes toward women, and have been doing so for more than a hundred years, but their attitudes must undergo this final change; namely, that where they may have retained any doubts about the right of women to complete equality as a human being and as a citizen they must shed their doubts and freely grant women that right. And this means not only constitutionally and before the law but in all human relationships on the interpersonal plane. The first large-scale step in the cooperation of men with women will be achieved when men make available to women their natural right to be what they want to be. It is a debt that men owe women, and payment is long overdue. The accumulated interest on the debt is enormous. Women don't expect to be paid the interest, compound or simple; which is all the more reason men should assume the obligation to discharge their debt and pay at least some of the interest by cooperating to the fullest in helping women to achieve complete emancipation from their long period of subjection to men.

As men aid women to emancipate themselves, so will women aid men to emancipate themselves from the confusions that have prevented them from realizing the best that is within them. Mutual aid is the principle by which all human beings must live if they are to live most efficiently and most happily. Women will not assist men in the dual task of emancipating women and emancipating themselves if they continue to play the role of clinging vines or half-men. Let women be themselves. In human relationships it is much more important to *be* the right person than to expect others to be so.

In a hostile, warring world women alone preserve the understanding of love. It is time for them to realize this; it is time for them to take the world back into their arms so that once again men may know what it means to live within the bosom of their family. Men can afford to be magnanimous; they can, in justice, be little less. Women must have the wisdom to recognize that justice is on their side, and to be generous—they could not be more; for women owe it not only to themselves, but to men, to their children, to civilization, to realize themselves, to be what it is in their nature to be, and not be content to remain what they have in so many cases become. Women play a very large role in determining the behavior of men toward themselves. Women must, therefore, take thought, and grasp the opportunity that is offered to help their men to help them achieve equality.

A democracy is as strong as its weakest links, and among the weakest links is the position of woman. It was Abraham Lincoln who said: "As I would not be a *slave*, so I would not be a *master*. This expresses my idea of democracy—whatever differs from this, to the extent of the difference, is no democracy." What is the extent of the difference between women and men in our democracy? The answer to the question will provide us with something of the measure of the changes that must be brought about—changes largely in the status of women—before we can speak of having a full democracy. Men and women must become partners in the greatest of democratic enterprises—the making of a democratic world; and a democratic world can be made only by persons who are themselves truly democratic. To label oneself democratic is not enough: one must *be* democratic.

Neither peace nor equilibrium can be achieved in a society in which the relationships between the sexes are out of balance. Most women and men wish to see a balance achieved, but they don't know quite how to bring it about. How is one to deal with the innumerable little and big problems that must be solved before progress can be made? Women are discontented with their lot—not all of them, but enough to constitute for them and for society a very real problem. Men feel that all is not well, and that something ought to be done about it—but what?

13.

Changing Traditions

DISCONTENT IS THE MOTHER of progress. Necessity is the mother of invention. And since discontent is almost a necessary condition of the life of the average educated woman of our day, progress and invention in the area of woman's place in the world are inevitable. The changes will come gradually but inevitably. The important thing is to see that we don't make too many mistakes; though we should avoid precipitancy we should not worry too much about wrecking the machinery of traditional social organization by exceeding the speed limit of rational inquiry; there need be no concern on that score, for we can expect the inertia of tradition to continue in the great tradition of tradition; namely, to act as a governor upon those who may be inclined to accelerate beyond the speed limit.

The educated woman in the Western world finds herself faced with a peculiarly complex dilemma. She is educated to appreciate and to contribute to the world in which she lives in a much broader capacity than that of wife and mother. She wants to be a good wife and mother, but she also wants to participate in a significant manner in the work of the world outside the home. She subscribes completely to the view that the home is the most influential environmental factor in the molding of the human personality. She wants the love of her husband and children and the shared responsibility of making good human beings of her children, but she also feels that she has capacities and abilities that cry out for exercise and for the discipline of using her mind to some useful purpose outside the home. But how can she be a good mother, a good wife, a good housekeeper, and have a job outside the home too?

I don't know whether anyone has ever given the answer to this question which I shall shortly give. I can only express the hope that its simplicity will not be too startling, or that it will not be thought too silly or impractical.

There still exists a general feeling that the married woman worker constitutes something of a problem. A married woman, it has been traditionally held, is the wife of her husband; her duty is to minister to his needs and to those of their children. The husband's duty is to provide for the family; it is the wife's to look after the family. Many married women, and particularly those who have enjoyed the benefits of a college education, find the traditional view of the occupational roles of husband and wife too one-sided. Certainly, a wife should fulfill the obligations that are traditionally expected of her, but she should also have a right to a life of her own. If a married woman wishes to work, she should be encouraged to do so. For a married woman to be gainfully employed outside the home is in no way incompatible with her being a good wife and a good mother; millions of married working women constitute living proof of the contrary.

The changes that have been going on during the last fifty years in the occupational roles of women will, no doubt, come as a great surprise to many who read these pages. Here are a few statistics. In 1870 less than two million women worked for pay in the United States; this was 18 percent of all women of working age, and 15 percent of all working people. In 1940 the number of working women was 14 million, 27 percent of all women of working age, and 25 percent of all working people. In 1947 there were 16½ million working women, 30 percent of the women of working age, and 28 percent of the working people of this country. In 1948 over 17¼ million women worked, 31 percent of the women of working age. In 1952 there were nearly 20 million working women, 33 percent of the women of working age, and over 31 percent of the working people of the United States. About one out of three mothers was in the labor force in 1965 as compared with less than one out of ten in 1940. The population of the United States as of 1972 was 203 million; of this number 107 million were female (51.2%) and 102 million were male (48.8%). The total noninstitutional population of females 16 years and over was 76 million compared with 70 million males. In 1972 there were over 33 million women workers in the United States, of whom 12.7 million were working mothers with children under eighteen years of age. These working mothers constituted 37 percent of the total number of women in the labor force and 35 percent of all mothers in the population.

Now consider the following facts: in 1900 there were, for every 100 working women, 328 full-time housewives; in 1940, 225; in 1945, owing to war conditions, only 154; and in 1950, 200. Particularly interesting are the age distribution and marital status of working women. In 1952 there were 11½ million single and 36 million married women in the population of the United States. In 1940 there were 1½ million more single than married women working for pay; in 1947 this relation was reversed; there were for the first time 1½ million more married than single women working. In 1952 there were nearly 2½ million more married than single women working. In addition there were more than 3½ million husbandless (widowed, divorced, separated) "married" women working. Thus in 1952 there were 12¼ million married working women in the United States, constituting about 55 percent of all female workers in the United States. In 1940 30 percent of all women workers were married and 48 percent were single. In 1964 these figures had changed to 62 and 23 percent respectively—a remarkable change reflecting the higher marriage rates, among other things. In 1972 these percentages remained about the same.

In 1900 there were less than 800,000 married women workers; in 1940 their number had risen to 5 million; in 1947 to 7½ million; and in 1952 to more than 8¾ million; that is to say, one out of every four married women worked for pay. In 1965, 15,790,000 married women worked for pay, that is, nearly three out of five. In 1972 this figure had risen to 20,749,000, or 42.1 percent of women (over 16 years) in the population.

Now, what is so highly interesting about these figures is that the increase in the number of working women from 1940 to 1965, amounting to 10 million, was due to the married women or women over thirty-five years of age. Part of the increase was undoubtedly attributable to the conditions brought about by World War II, when so many men were away from home and many women found themselves with the opportunity to take a full-time job and did so. But the trend has continued to the present day. In the same period, 1940 to 1965, the number of working girls less than twenty years old increased by more than one-third of a million, while from 1940 to 1952 the number in the age group from twenty to thirty-four years, the childbearing years, decreased by one-third million. By 1965 this same age group exceeded the number working in 1940 by 1.3 million.

Two-thirds of the female labor force in 1972 was composed of married women living with their husbands; more than a fifth of the women who work are mothers with children under eighteen years; that is, more than 4 million of the women working in 1949 had children younger than eighteen years of age. Of these 4 million working mothers, more than 1½ million had children younger than school age. The others had children over six only. In 1965 these figures were respectively 9.7 million and 3¾ million, and in 1972 mothers with children under 18 numbered 12,682,000, of which 4½ million had children under 6 years of age, the totals being:

All working mothers	12,700,000
Mothers with children under 6	4,438,000
Mothers with children 6 to 17	8,300,000

The great proportion of these working mothers were married women living with their husbands, and not widowed, divorced, or separated. Less than one million of the mothers who worked did not have husbands:

All working mothers	12,700,000
Married women with husbands	10,452,000
Widowed, divorced, or separated	2,300,000

This group of working mothers represents one-third of all women who have children under eighteen:

All mothers	29,600,000
Working mothers	12,700,000
Mothers not in labor force	16,900,000

That women can hold an outside job and run a home too is evident from these figures. The tables also demonstrate a trend that will continue in the indicated direction: More and more married women will be going to work, even in the childbearing age group from twenty to thirty-four.

The number of married women who are outearning their husbands is also increasing. In 1960 the figure was 5.7 percent. In 1970 the figure had risen to 7.4 percent or in 3.2 million families. Of these 22 percent were in clerical occupations and 21 percent in professional or technical fields.

What are the effects upon the family when the mother becomes a working woman? Of course, no generalized answer to cover all cases can be given. Such studies as we have that throw any light on the subject point uniformly in the same direction. The married woman worker has generally learned to systematize her housework so well that she experiences no difficulty. In one study, made in Philadelphia, over 62 percent of the working mothers maintained either that there had been no effect on the quality of their household management or that their housekeeping had actually improved. Many of these working mothers had learned the value of order and routine so well that their homes, in these respects, would compare very favorably with the best-run homes of nongainfully employed housewives. Similar results are reported in an English study.

But what of the effects upon the children? As the figures given above show, most mothers don't go to work until their children are six or more years old. Even so, the children will generally not be at home without their mother for more than two or three hours. They get out of school at three or three-thirty, and mother returns after five. Mother would not see significantly more of her children, except at the very end of this period, even if she stayed at home. It is perhaps not difficult to understand why the working mother is often happier with her children than the mother who, having become progressively fatigued and exhausted with the routine chores of the day, awaits the return of the children from school with some trepidation. Her loneliness during the greater part of the day, when husband and children are away, compares very unfavorably with the kind of stimulation that the working mother receives from her workaday experience with the outside world. Of the two, the working mother may, in general, have the advantage, as a mother and a wife, on her side.

A working mother may, however, work too hard, and she may be in no state to resume the cares of a household upon returning from her work. Of course, this is highly undesirable, and no mother should engage in exhausting work. It is unnecessary to deal here with the exploitation of women as cheap labor, unequal pay for the same job, and discrimination against women workers. These practices are steadily losing ground and will continue to lose ground. They are regrettable, and an unfortunate reflection upon the character of many men.

Thus far, all I have attempted to do in this chapter is to show that more and more women, and particularly married women, are working, and will continue to work, outside the home. It is a trend that no one can stop: the married working woman is here to stay. For the most part she works for the same reason that the married man does: to help support the family.

During the Second World War the Women's Bureau of the Department of Labor conducted a study among 13,000 working women employed in all sorts of industries. More than half the married women planned to continue working in peacetime. Among the reasons they gave were: to support themselves and others, 57 percent;

to save money in order to help buy a home or educate children, 21 percent; because they liked to, and because of the independence that working gave them, 22 percent.

Now, compare the statements of the unmarried women. Eighty-six percent of the single women planned to continue working in peacetime, and of these 96 percent gave as their reason support of themselves or others; 2 percent were saving for a special purpose; and only 2 percent said they worked because they liked doing so!

In other words, after a taste of domesticity, a fourth of the women who looked forward to marriage find a job outside the home a refreshing experience. There can be little doubt that increasing numbers of married women will continue to do so—and for much the same reasons that men do; it gives them a change, much needed stimulation, the acquaintance and friendship of persons one would otherwise never have known, the sense of doing something that is contributing to making the world go round.

Men escape the chores of domesticity, seeing neither their wives nor their children for the greater part of the day. Hence, if father is away for the greater part of the day, someone else must take care of the children and the household. There are many men who still consider it an affront to their ego when their wives suggest that they would like to go out and work too. A man is traditionally the support of his family—so the story goes. But women have been working for ages, on the land, in agricultural and industrial cooperatives, taking in piecework in the home, and the like, and in this way they have helped support the family. Until the advent of machinery many women of the poorer families, even in large urban centers, helped to support the family. It has largely been a middle- and upper-class prejudice, now rapidly losing ground, that women shouldn't work. It is an issue upon which, after the children are sufficiently grown up, fewer men would quarrel with their wives than would have done so twenty years ago.

It is an interesting fact that while men will take every opportunity of emphasizing that it is a mother's task to look after the children, they will neglect to observe that a father is a parent too and that his responsibility to his children is no less great than his wife's. Father usually relieves himself of the responsibility for the upbringing of the children on the plea that practically all his time is consumed in the process of making a living; and having satisfied himself—if no one else—on this point, he complacently feels that everyone understands. But nobody understands—least of all himself. The fact is that, in general, men don't like domestic responsibilities and would do almost anything to avoid them. The traditional dispensation that enables them to get out of the house for the greater part of the day, and thus escape the incubus of domestic chores, is worth any sacrifice. Not that the average man doesn't love his home and family —but he loves dishwashing, laundering, changing diapers and baby clothes, and cleaning the house and making the beds so much less that he is willing to give up almost everything to his family in exchange for his "freedom"!

Certainly, the American husband is a great help around the house, and he's a fine fellow. European women sigh for American husbands because, as they rightly say, they are so kind. Good. American men probably do make the kindest and most generous husbands. But even so, they may be accused of running away. They may be accused of running away from their responsibilities as husbands and fathers, of vacating the privilege of participating fully in the growth and development of their families; of running out on the most rewarding experience of life, the molding and making of the character of another human being, in the process of which the husband and wife provide the life they brought into being with the skills and techniques for being human.

When men abandon the upbringing of their children to their wives, a loss is suffered by everyone, but perhaps most of all by themselves. For what they lose is the possibility of growth in themselves for being human which the stimulation of bringing up one's children gives. Pearl Buck has put what I want to say so beautifully that I should like to quote her:

It is perfectly true that women do not see enough of men here, and that the children suffer from the lack of influence of men upon them in home and school. But men lose more. They lose very much when they relegate home and children to women. They lose fun and the excitement of growing, developing life—life which they have had a part in creating. But they lose something deeper than that. They lose touch with the source of the life itself, which is deep in the very process of living with a woman and the children a man has created with her. When he lives not there but in his office, in his work, among other men, he is strangling the roots of his own being. If he can comprehend fully the one woman and can help her to comprehend him, they are both fulfilled. When they enlarge the mutual comprehension to include children, then the universe is within their grasp and they cannot be disturbed. They have life in their time.[1]

"They have life in their time." In our time, however, most men miss this quintessential experience of life, or partake of it fitfully. Next to the loss of mother love, it is the greatest loss a man can suffer; and in a very deep and significant sense it may be said that no man who has failed to take an active part in the rearing of chil-

[1] *Of Men and Women* (New York: John Day Company, 1941), pp. 55–56.

dren ever develops as a complete human being. Somehow women do not seem to suffer in quite the same way as men do from the effects of such privation, but suffer to some extent they do.

What, then, is the poor working man to do? After his arrival home is he to spend the remainder of the children's waking time with them? Should he spend a good part of his weekend with them? And what of the working mother? Should she do likewise?

It will be generally agreed that such cut-and-dried apportionments of time do not represent the best possible thing for the children; yet for some time to come many children, after they have passed the age of early childhood, will receive little more of their parents' time. I suggest that, granting the importance of parents for the development of good mental health, some better arrangement could be conceived whereby parents and children might enjoy a greater amount of time together. Our society would do well to consider the effects of the changing roles of parents, and to plan for the future in the light of these trends. I have a suggestion to make that, though at first it would involve certain practical difficulties and readjustments, would, I believe, solve many of the problems that bedevil both women and men and seriously affect our society. It is, otherwise, a very simple idea—too simple, I will be told, I'm sure.

I suggest that for married persons the working day be limited, on a voluntary basis, to half the normal working hours, that is, to four hours a day. Such an arrangement would immediately make it possible for each of the parents to spend not only a great deal more time with their children but with each other, and would result in other untold benefits to our society. It is not being suggested that such an arrangement would automatically produce these effects. In the majority of cases, one may speculate, it would greatly help. I do not think that one need give serious thought to the possibility that a certain proportion of fathers would take advantage of the opportunity thus made available to spend more time at the race track or in playing pool. Working hours could be arranged so that husband and wife could work the same hours, either in the morning or in the afternoon, or one could work in the morning and the other in the afternoon. Thus at least one of the parents would be at home a good part of the day, or both of them would.

Making more time available to young parents would not in itself solve any problems; it is not time but the uses to which one puts it which are important. I am assuming that educational changes paralleling the changes here suggested will have occurred which will prepare young parents to put their new inheritance of time to healthy constructive uses. Wisely used, the bounty of increased time would make the solution of innumerable family problems so much easier; it would contribute substantially to the solution of the problem of leisure and assist our whole society to take on a less tired, less feverish look.

Working married couples have greatly increased since the prewar period. The number of couples in the population of the United States with the husband the head of the family increased from 26% million in 1940 to almost 34 million in 1950. Of these couples, the proportion with both spouses in the labor force increased from 11 percent (almost 3 million couples) in 1940 to 22 percent (more than 7⅓ million couples) in 1950. Actually, there were more than 8 million couples with husband and wife in the labor force in 1950, but for about two-thirds of a million of these couples the husband was not the family head (as, for example, among young couples living with their parents). By 1965 the number of working couples had risen to 13.5 million—

32 percent of all couples in the population. In 1972 there were 21 million working couples, or 45 percent of all husband–wife families in the population.

It has been calculated that no one in our society need work more than three hours a day in a five-day working week. All the work, and more, that is done today on a full week's employment could be done on a three-hour-a-day week of five workdays. I think we will eventually arrive at such a workday, but I am not suggesting it now. I am not suggesting that the five-day working week or the eight-hour day be abolished; such arrangements may be retained for unmarried persons and for all married persons on a voluntary basis. I am suggesting that as soon as women and men marry they be given the privilege of working only half a day, say a total of four hours each of the five days of the week. When children arrive, the mother should not work for at least two years but should devote herself to her child and home; the husband should have the freedom to work no more than half a day during this period and thereafter. Women and children could, indeed, have life in their time. And I see such working and family arrangements as these, as well as other benefits, as the product of the approach of the sexes toward a better understanding of each other.

I am quite aware that the four-hour working day will be dismissed by many as impractical and that it will be greeted by others with derision. I should like to remind any such readers that many of the impracticalities of yesterday are the realities of today. Not so long ago many workers were laboring eighteen and sixteen hours a day, while the twelve-hour working day is a matter of the very recent past. The twelve-hour working day has been reduced to an eight-hour day, and in some cases to a six-hour working day. There were those who thought that the introduction of such short working hours would ruin our economy. The best answer to them is the economic history of the United States.

Let us be fair and try to see whether the suggested four-hour working day has any merit at all. No one could expect it to be put into practice on an extended scale, and all of a sudden, as it were; but do let us try it on a small, experimental scale at first, in various parts of the country and under varying conditions, and let us fairly judge the results. If the results are satisfactory, let us extend the four-hour working day for married couples. If the results are unsatisfactory, let us drop the whole idea. I am willing to predict that when it is tried and examined, workers who have had a four-hour working day to look forward to will on the whole be found to be more efficient than those who have to contemplate a working day twice as long. Anyone who has had any experience in such matters will, I think, agree. In considering the balance of incentives to work, students of industrial life have uniformly found that the most important factor in a worker's efficiency is his happiness at his work. In this, as in so many other matters, the secret of happiness lies not so much in doing what one likes as in liking what one has to do.

The advantages of the four-hour working day are innumerable and far-reaching; the effects of such an arrangement could alter the face of our whole civilization and contribute to the improvement of human relations in the most effective and wholesome of ways. It would give men and women, for the first time in their lives, the time they have never enjoyed for doing something constructive about human relations. It would give them the time for fulfilling the primary function of life: living. As it is, most people haven't sufficient time to live, and time is a very necessary and perishable commodity in the process of living.

I conceive that the most important function of the four-hour day for family couples is to make more time available for the parents, and particularly the father, to be with their children and with each other. Even if one parent works in the morning and one in the afternoon, each will be in a much more fresh and happy state of mind than he would be at the conclusion of an eight-hour day. Parents would profit vastly more from being together under such a budgeting of their time than if they worked an eight-hour day. One could easily fill a large book by setting out the advantages of the four-hour day, and I hope someone will do so. I do not, however, think that the advantages need be enumerated here; the reader, in reflecting upon the proposal, will readily see many of them for himself. Once he grants the desirability of trying the experiment, a way must be found to do so. In certain groups where conditions are favorable, as among teachers and in academic groups, such an experiment would be quite feasible. In the business world special arrangements would have to be made in order to conduct such an experiment. Indeed, the first steps in this direction will probably be taken by an enlightened private industry. And there is no reason why a movement for a "Four-Hour Working Day for the Married" couldn't get under way. I am convinced that genuinely civilized living will not come about until, among other things, the four-hour working day is available to everyone.

In general, evidence indicates that no mother should abandon her child for a job before the child is six years old. Experts at the Midcentury White House Conference on Children and Youth agreed in its fact-finding report that such abandonment was undesirable. They said: "It may well be questioned whether most mothers can, without undue strain, carry a full-time job and still give responsive and attentive care to the physical and emotional needs of small children. The first six years have been shown to be crucial years for the child, who would seem to need a substantial share of the mother's time and attention during this period." Hence, short of the four-hour working day, I can see no satisfactory way of solving the problems of the mother of the preschool child, of the mother who wants to be a mother to her child and who also wishes to work outside the home. But until the four-hour day or some such working-day arrangement comes into being, such mothers will have to resort to mother substitutes, nursery schools, and day care centers. These can never be adequate substitutes for a mother who wants to be a mother. Men must learn to understand these facts as well as women.

As men begin to understand women's true value, and rid themselves of the myths that have been traditionally foisted upon them, they will come to view their relationship to women as a partnership conferring mutual benefits, as well as benefits upon all who come within the orbit of their influence. The freeing of women and increasing respect for them will mean the freeing of, and increasing respect for, men. Men need not fear that women will be transformed into men or that men will turn into women—there are certain biological arrangements in each of the sexes which will effectually prevent such development. On the contrary, each of the sexes will for the first time function as completely as it has hitherto functioned incompletely, for each will have, for the first time, a full opportunity to realize itself according to its own nature and *not* according to the nature that has been forced upon it.

What do the schools teach concerning the sexes? Largely what is taken for granted. But the schools could be a most powerful influence in readjusting the sexes to each other in the light of our newer knowledge and of the great benefits that will accrue from the application of our knowledge. Such facts and ideas as I have set forth in this book should be a matter of staple discussion in our schools and colleges, and evaluated for what they are worth. From the very beginning children of opposite sex should be educated to understand each other; they should not be left to pick up the traditional myths they find so freely floating about in their culture. The essential human state is harmony, cooperativeness; our culture has managed to produce a complex separateness and lack of understanding between the sexes. Much effort will be required to break down this separateness, but I know of no better way to accomplish this than by education—the education of the sexes *for* each other, not in opposition to each other.

An ounce of example is worth a pound of precept any day. But in view of the probability that the examples will be rather slow in developing, education concerning the sexes will always remain necessary. The sooner we begin teaching the facts—and not only the facts, but the practice of their implications in human relations—the better.

The climate of opinion concerning the status and the relations of the sexes in recent years has undergone so favorable a change that the idea, for example, of a woman running for the Vice Presidency of the United States is no longer as inconceivable as it was a few years ago. This marks a definite advance; but should it be suggested that a woman might stand as a candidate for the Presidency of the United States a loud chorus of dissenting voices will be heard throughout the land. But the number of those who will not join in the chorus has enormously increased. In 1973 there were no women in the Senate and only 15 in the House. During Mr. Truman's administration our delegate to the United Nations was a woman, and so were two of the alternates. The Federal Security Administrator, under

President Eisenhower, was a woman; so was the Treasurer of the United States, and so was the Director of the Mint; two of our ambassadors were women, and the Assistant Secretary of Defense was a woman. It is commonly acknowledged that the women in these posts have, even by male standards, done quite well. Indeed, American women in general have done extremely well, and this in itself constitutes one of the greatest tributes that one can pay to American men. Men have the women they deserve.

It is estimated that women cast more than one-half the ballots in national elections and yet full constitutional rights are not yet theirs. One of the most notable ways in which women can exercise their influence is through the ballot, principally by helping to elect to the legislatures of the land men *and* women who are sympathetic to their cause. The Ninety-Third Congress in 1973 opened with 15 women and 522 men on its rolls, and this even though there are six million more women than men in the United States. This can scarcely be called proportional representation. It is up to women to change this state of affairs; and it cannot be too emphatically stated that unless they exert themselves to bring about a fairer representation of their sex in Congress, no one else will. The government of this land, of every land, needs the brains, the ability, and the understanding of women. It should be a self-imposed obligation upon women to take politics more seriously than they have in the past. Women have an important contribution to make to their society, and one of the best ways to do so is through politics. Let it be remembered that politics is the complete science of human nature, the science through which human nature is ordered. If the world is to be remade, human nature will have to be remade, a task in which women must always play the leading role.

Who is to remake the world? It is a proper question to ask in a book of this sort, which has been written not simply to throw some light on the relations between the sexes with especial reference to man's injustice to women, but as part of the larger task of helping human beings to understand themselves better, to understand more fully how they came to be the way they are now, and what they can do about changing the conditions that make men and women function as unhappily as they frequently do at present. Who is to remake the world? Those who begin remaking the world by remaking themselves; those who will help future generations remake the world nearer the heart's desire by assisting to free the next generation, and the generations to follow, from the myths upon which their parents were bred; those who will make the truth available to the next generation in a self-actualizing way. They will do so not simply by stating the facts but by incorporating them into the lives of those who are to be the future citizens of the world in a vital and meaningful manner.

Women are already exercising a considerable influence in the realm of political and social action, an influence that is so conspicuously for the good that one can only hope women will not long delay entering both the governments of their states and of their country in larger numbers than they have so far done. Not only their communities, their states, and their country need their help; the world also needs it. I have seen the ideas and action women have to offer in a multiplicity of different roles, and I have found them good. I recommend them to the attention of my fellow men, and particularly to those women who are wanting in sufficient faith in their own sex.

In national elections women's votes will increasingly come to play a major role.

In the field of education it will not be long before

women are admitted in greater numbers as teachers in the colleges and universities, where, it is to be hoped and expected, their verbal abilities will reduce some of the dead weight of boredom that has afflicted so many campuses for too many generations! Pernicious academia is at present largely a disorder due to academic masculine inbreeding. Most of our higher institutions of learning have a *numerus clausus*, a usually unwritten but in some instances written limitation, on the number of women that can be admitted to academic faculty rank. Discrimination against women teachers at the higher academic levels is still gross and crude, but it too will pass.

Another anachronism that, it is to be hoped, will not endure much longer is the college that caters to one sex only. Such institutions represented hangovers from an earlier period. They have done noble service, but their day is over. They can make a great contribution to American education by converting themselves into co-educational institutions. It does neither young men nor young women any good to be locked up in monasteries and nunneries during the years when they should be enjoying each other's society.

Perhaps when the sexes have developed a better understanding of each other, men will not only cease to be appointed presidents of universities for the reasons that usually bring men that high privilege, but women will be given the opportunity to serve equally with men in such capacities.

On school boards and boards of higher education women already play a distinguished role. Parent-Teacher associations throughout the country are almost entirely the doing of American women, and their influence for good in the schools and in the community, and thus throughout the land, has been incalculable.

Women are the cultural torchbearers in America; and even in the darkest parts of the land, wherever a gleam of light is seen it is usually cast from a source upheld by the hand of a woman.

14.

Woman's Task

IT WAS A VICTORIAN SAYING that the last thing man would civilize would be woman. This was, of course, intended as a criticism of woman's alleged refractoriness. The Victorian male ensconced in his citadel of infallibility, certain of his own superiority and of the female's inferiority, employed the myth of female inferiority as the "explanation" of the female's unyieldingness to the blandishments of civilization. Perhaps it is a fortunate thing for the world that women, by being prevented from "yielding" to men's interest in things mechanical and material, have had to pay so much more attention to people, and therefore, in the twentieth century, are better equipped to solve the problems of mankind than most men.

Civilization is the art of being kind, an art at which women excel.

Shall I be told that women can be quite as unkind and as bigoted as many men? Indeed they can, and a great many other things too; but it is not natural for them to be so, any more than it is natural for men to be so. In general, women tend to retain a sympathy for the other which so many men seem to lose. Men have done themselves the greatest disservice in their traditional attitudes toward women, for in being unfair to women they have been unfair to themselves, and have crippled the development of their potentialities, for tenderness especially, and for kindness in general. In the Western world there has been a taboo on tenderness as a male trait. One of the primary tasks of women will be to remove the taboo, for it is largely by the warmth of their own tenderness that the long ice age of man's emotions will be thawed.

The natural superiority of women is a biological fact, and a socially unacknowledged reality. The facts have been available for more than half a century, but in a male-dominated world, in which the inflation of the male ego has been dependent upon the preservation of the myth of male superiority, the significance of those facts has simply been denied attention. When the history of the subject comes to be written, this peculiar omission will no doubt serve as yet another forcible illustration that men see only what and how they want to see.

Male superiority has been dependent upon female inferiority, and as long as everyone believed that the male was naturally superior to the female neither men nor women were disposed to see the facts for what they were. Beliefs and prejudices, especially when they are sanctioned by age and fortified by "experience," are often so much more convincing than facts. But facts, as Mr. Pecksniff said, "is facts"; and the truth does have a way of asserting itself and of eventually prevailing. I hope the facts have been made sufficiently clear in this book to cause the reader to reflect upon the possibility that women are naturally far better endowed than has hitherto been generally understood or allowed.

Science is not a matter of private whim or personal

prejudice; it is a public method of drawing rigorously systematic conclusions from facts that have been confirmed by observation and experiment. The facts cited in this book supporting the thesis of the natural superiority of women will be considered and evaluated by scientists and laymen alike. All that the author can claim to have done is to set out the facts and offer his interpretation of them; as a scientist I have done my best to ensure their accuracy and to offer a sound interpretation of their meaning. It now remains for readers to evaluate critically what I have done. In the presence of startling ideas, the truly scientific attitude is neither the will to believe nor the will to disbelieve, but the will to investigate.

I consider the theme of this book to be a most important one, for I am convinced, and I hope the reader will agree, that good relations between the sexes are basic to the development of good human relations in all societies. This should be obvious, yet men do not behave as if it were. Is it too much to hope that the claims herein made for the natural superiority of women will shake men out of their complacent acceptance of the present position of the sexes? If I had thought that that was too much to hope, I should not have written this book. It is to be expected that there will be some discussion of my contentions, and that is highly desirable; for the more we talk about the relations of the sexes, and the more informed we are while doing so, the greater will be our progress toward establishing better relations between them.

I hope it is clear to every reader that, in stating the case for the natural superiority of women, I have not been trying to degrade men by upgrading women—nothing has been further from my mind. Nevertheless, I have been constantly aware that a book with a title such as this, arguing the case as it does, would lead some persons to believe that I am attempting to knock men down by elevating women above them. I cannot state too strongly that this has never been part of my intention. My intention has been to state the facts about women in order to correct the myths that have for too long served in place of the facts. As we have seen in the preceding pages, the facts prove that woman is biologically the superior organism, superior in the sense of enjoying, by virtue of her biological traits, a higher survival value than the male. These facts should forever dispose of the myth of the female's physical inferiority to the male. Muscular strength should not be confused with constitutional strength. Constitutionally the female is the stronger sex.

It is either a fact or it is not that women are biologically superior to men. It is quite understandable that there will be many who will argue that we have had more than enough of talk of "superiority" and "inferiority," and, indeed, we have when it is a matter of comparing populations and "races," [1] but in the comparison of the sexes the facts are indisputably in favor of the female. The sensible thing is to consider the meaning of those facts, and the social action they indicate.

With respect to psychological and social qualities, the facts again, it seems to me, prove that women are superior to men. The proof here, too, is by the measure of our test of biological superiority, for women, by their greater loving kindness and humanity, tend to confer survival benefits upon all who come within their orbit more frequently than do men.

Women are the bearers, the nurturers of life; men have more often tended to be the curtailers, the de-

---

[1] Ashley Montagu, *Man's Most Dangerous Myth: The Fallacy of Race*, 4th ed. (New York: World Publishing Co., 1964).

stroyers of life. Clearly, as both men and women are necessary for the creation and continuation of human life, the fundamental pattern of cooperation that is here biologically indicated between the sexes is the one that should prevail.

Though it is a platitude to say that the sexes complement each other, men have not, on the whole, accepted the principle of complementarity of the sexes; they have insisted that women be the "inferiors." It has been shown in this book that women are, on the whole, the superior organisms. Perhaps, swallowing this pill, together with their pride, as gracefully as they can, men may more easily hereafter be able to accept that the sexes should complement each other. Each of the sexes has a great deal to learn and *unlearn* from the other; they can best do so by getting together on an "equal though different" basis. In other words, the sexes need to learn the truth about each other, to take stock in each other, and know each other's weaknesses and strengths.

Men will have to give up their belief in masculine superiority and learn that superiority is where it resides, regardless of a person's sex. Men will have to accept that in so far as biological superiority is concerned women have the edge on them; but there is not the least reason why this should upset the male ego. On the other hand, men should congratulate themselves that the mothers of their children are so well endowed. It has often been remarked that if men had to have babies, few of them would survive the ordeal. All men should be eternally grateful to women for undertaking the task. How good and pleasing a thought it is that women should be constitutionally stronger than men; that is as it should be, and that is as it is. The natural superiority of women is something for which we should all be grateful. When we recognize it for what it is, the biological safeguard of the race, we shall be all the more ready to cherish and respect it.

Human beings differ greatly in their abilities but practically not at all along sex lines; that is to say, abilities are not determined by sex. Abilities are functions of persons, *not* of groups or classes. Hence, so far as abilities are concerned both sexes should be afforded equal opportunities to realize their potentialities, and the judgment of their abilities should not be prejudiced by any bias of sex.

Women should no longer accept a state of permanent male patronage. They should no longer permit their world to be exclusively run by men.

Women must be granted complete equality with men, for only when this has been done will they fully be able to realize themselves. No one can doubt that such equality will eventually be granted women. The important point is, the sooner it is done, the better; the sooner men cooperate with women to accomplish this inevitable change, the sooner will the great contributions that women have to make to humanity become creative realities redounding to the benefit of all.

All human beings should enjoy the rights that are theirs by virtue of their being human, and not one iota of their rights should ever be abridged on the ground of sex; but to secure them women will have to labor hard. It cannot be too often repeated that they will have to do most of the work themselves in improving their status. Getting laws passed will not be enough; the long hard pull will be to achieve full recognition and acceptance of their abilities in all phases of national and international life.

It is by becoming actively participating members of their society through their work that women will make greatest progress. The work of the world has for too long been the exclusive preserve of the male; there is every reason why it should not continue to be so. The male has sought to keep the management of the world in his own hands because it has satisfied a deep need within him—the need to feel superior. Women must help men to learn that working in cooperation rather than in conflict is the best support for their egos which men can receive. Men can go no further without women; they need the help of women in balancing the budget of effort and accomplishment; and women need to realize that among their unique contributions to society is what is so often called "the woman's point of view." A full-rounded judgment of most human endeavors is best achieved when it represents the combined wisdom of man and woman. Surely, most people who have made a success of their marriage are aware of this. Always remembering that happiness in marriage often means being unhappy together.

Because there is too much economics in our society and not enough understanding of human relations, women can make another major contribution by introducing a greater understanding and practice of human relations in the business world. As one businessman, speaking for many others, put it impressively and succinctly, "You should have seen this place before we employed women. They've civilized it." A scarcely higher tribute could be paid to women's capacity for human relations. Human societies must be based on human relations first, and economic activities must be a function of human relations—not the other way round. This is an area in which women have heroic work to do. The genius for humanity which women naturally possess and develop so highly as mothers will find material to work upon in every phase of life.

The most important of women's tasks is the making of human beings in cooperation with their husbands. In this happiest and most rewarding of all labors of love, women bear a great responsibility, for they hold no less than the future in their hands. Because mothers are closer to their children than fathers, they must of necessity play a more basic role in the growth and development of their children. The importance of mother love for the development of human beings healthy in mind and body is fundamental. Both mothers and fathers must love themselves and each other if they are to love their children as they need to be loved. Love, indeed, is not all, but it *is* almost all. Women must be free to give their children the love they require, and men must assist them to do so. Men must understand how much they have to learn from women, as well as how much they have to teach them. Here, indeed, is the great opportunity for mutual aid. The sexes are happiest, and will always be happiest, when they work and play together, not only in rearing children and making homes but when they are helping each other to realize the best that is within them. Such a mutually creative and enlarging relationship need not be restricted to married life but can be extended to all the relationships between men and women. There is no reason why we cannot be of help to each other in everything.

Men should give up arguing about women and start thinking jointly with them. To this end the education of the sexes must receive a thorough but readily feasible revision. The sexes should be educated for each other, with opportunities for education that are in every way equal. The late Alfred North Whitehead described education as the guidance of the person toward a comprehension of the art of life. Every person embodies an adventure of existence, and the art of life consists in the guidance of this adventure, an adventure in which men and women must participate equally. The prime business of a democracy, the great democratic task of

men and women, is not the making of things, not even
the making of money, but the making of human beings.

The portents are good. During the last fifty years
great strides have been made at an accelerating pace.
There is every reason to believe that women, together
with men, will continue to make progress in the right
direction. It has been said that the belief in progress is
the wine of the present poured out as a libation to the
future. The expression of optimistic hopes is not enough.
The progress that women have made has been largely
their own accomplishment, and such progress as they
make in future, it must be repeated, will be the result
largely of their own hard work.

It is the women who excel as women who will win
success for the cause of humanity and not the "phony
feminists" who behave as if they believe that by beating
men at their own jobs they thereby demonstrate their
own equality with men. The sexes should not compete;
they should cooperate and complement each other.
When they compete they do themselves and one another
a disservice. Women should not try to be like men, and
men should not try to be like women. That sounds almost like a platitude, yet how many women have realized
it? Can there be anything more egregious or pathetic
than the woman with close-cut hair and tailored suit
parroting the manner of the male? Is it not a curious
fact that apparently normal women will adopt such
manners, whereas few normal males ever seem to desire
to imitate the female? When we encounter a feminine
male we suspect—generally correctly—a somewhat abnormal psychological history. The "inferior" models
himself upon his "superior"; rarely does the "superior"
pattern himself after the model of the "inferior." "Phony
feminists" are rarely mistaken for anything other than
what they are: persons with inferiority feelings who are
attempting to compensate for their feeling of inferiority

as women. By behaving in this way "phony feminists" are false to themselves as women and, therefore, false to women and men, as to humanity.

Women no more serve the cause of humanity by aping men than Blacks do by aping Whites. A Black's dark skin is, in its own way, at least as beautiful as a "white" skin, yet so many Blacks have accepted the white imputation of inferiority that they would give anything to possess a white skin! This is perfectly understandable, but it is a falling into the very error that one should wish to avoid; namely, accepting the errors of judgment and conduct of "superiors" who have made one feel inferior. Women must avoid continuing to fall into this trap. Women must realize that they have been and are living in a patriarchal society, that men have tried to make them as they would have them be, and then convince them that as they have made them so it is natural for them to be—inferior to men. Women have been more or less deliberately tailored to the pattern preferred by men, and thus accustomed to thinking of themselves as men's inferiors; in being thus custommade, women have been deformed and wrested from their true life course to serve the misconceived needs of the male. The male has confused his needs, and he has badly confused women, but not half so badly as he has confused himself. Yet, though not half so confused as men, women are sufficiently so to go on repeating a pattern that turns out men who will uphold the old traditions. It is perfectly true that many men are what they are because they were raised by women— but, it should be added, by women who were raised according to masculine standards of what both a woman and a man should be. Such traditional standards are unsound, and women know this better than men because they are less confused than men, and because, as the mothers of mankind, they are its original lovers.

A serious and a heavy responsibility is placed upon women. Women suddenly find themselves in much the same position as the United States all at once finds itself in relation to the rest of the world. Almost too precipitately the United States finds itself the richest and the most powerful nation in the world, and its problem is the recognition of its responsibility to the rest of the world, the proper relation of its strength to the rest of the world's weakness. Similarly, the problem that woman will have increasingly to face is the sudden awareness of her strength in relation to man's weakness. Recognition of this problem will undoubtedly prove unbalancing to many women, but when all the sound and fury has died down the question will remain: What can women do to pull mankind through?

In the first place, women must learn to respect themselves as women and not to think of themselves, any longer than is necessary, as pale and submissive echoes of their alter egos. Respect must be based on self-knowledge and the knowledge of the high privilege of what it means to be a woman. When women understand what it really means, sociobiologically, to be a woman, in terms such as I have set out in this book, they can then confidently move out into the world and assume their rightful place in it. Not having been trusted for so long, many women have lost faith in themselves. Women need to recover that faith. Women need confidence in themselves and a fuller awareness of the responsibility that being a woman entails. In the second place, women must assume the obligation of fulfilling their responsibilities, *not* as subjects of men, but as equally important, if not the most important, members of the community of humanity. Women are the mothers of humanity; do not let us ever forget that or underemphasize its importance. What mothers are to their children, so will man be to man. What man has made of man, he has tried to make of woman; but he has never quite succeeded, for the mother that is in woman will keep expressing herself. Women must assume the full birthright of motherhood. I do not mean that all women must necessarily become the mothers of children—I use the term "mother" in a larger sense than that of the purely biological mother: to refer to the woman who extends her love to embrace every person and all mankind, to those qualities that are exemplified by the mother's love for her child but that are also applied to all persons and to all humanity. Women are the carriers of the true spirit of humanity—the love of the mother for her child. The preservation of that kind of love is the true function of women. And let me, at this point, endeavor to make it quite clear why I mean the love of a mother for her child and not the love of an equal for an equal, or any other kind of love.

Maternal love is the purest and at the same time the most efficient form of love because it is the most compassionate, because it is the most sympathetic, because it is the most understanding and the least censorious. Maternal love does not dispense justice; it neither condemns nor condones; it gives support while endeavoring to understand, and it never forsakes those who are dependent upon it. Maternal love is much more than just, for it functions as if it were aware that justice without love is not enough. Justice is love digested through rational calculation; love, more importantly, is justice adapted to the needs of the organism, and the maintenance of the organism then and thereafter in the warm ambience of its support. This, surely, is the kind of love we would wish to see prevail between human beings, rather than the kind of love that limits itself to the narrowest orbit and is conditional upon the fulfillment of certain strictly limited requirements.[2]

Why cannot we love our fellow human beings as mothers love their children? And why cannot we demonstrate this love toward them? Is there, would there be, anything wrong in loving our fellow human beings in this way? Indeed, I believe that there is not only nothing wrong with this way of loving human beings but that unless we learn so to love before much more time has passed we may not be able to love at all. It is the way of love in which human beings may live most successfully and happily and in optimum health, and it is the evolutionary destiny of human beings so to love each other. I believe that it is the unique function and destiny of women to teach men to live as if to live and love were one.

Perhaps there has never been a time in the history of men when all or most men loved each other as mothers love their children. We can be certain, however, that throughout the long range of human history mankind has been slowly, painfully, and gropingly finding its way toward discovery of itself, toward a way of life in which human beings will love one another as mothers love their children. Every religious and ethical system testifies to that fact, and as an anthropologist concerned with the study of human nature I see it as one of the great goals toward which human society is striving. Hence, the crucial importance of women in this evolutionary process, and the great necessity of becoming consciously aware of what has, for the most part, been attempting unconsciously to realize itself: the love of man for man.

True love is self-denying, so suffused with humility

2 See Ashley Montagu, *On Being Human*, 2nd ed. (New York: Hawthorn Books, 1967).

that those who exhibit it are not likely to dwell upon
its meaning. Woman knows what true love is; let her
not be tempted from her knowledge by the false idols
that man has created for her to worship. Woman must
stand firm and be true to her own inner nature; to yield
to the prevailing false conceptions of love, of unloving
love, is to abdicate her great evolutionary mission to
keep human beings true to themselves, to keep them
from doing violence to their inner nature, to help them
to realize their potentialities for being loving and cooperative. Were women to fail in this task, all hope for the
future of humanity would depart from the world.

> From women's eyes this doctrine I derive:
> They sparkle still the right Promethean fire;
> They are the books, the arts, the academes,
> That show, contain, and nourish all the world:
> Else, none at all in aught proves excellent.[3]

[3] Shakespeare, *Love's Labour's Lost*, iv–3.

Appendix:
U.N. Declaration
on Women's Rights

Following is the text of a declaration on discrimination against women, as adopted 7 November 1967 in the General Assembly:

The General Assembly,

Considering that the peoples of the United Nations have, in the Charter, reaffirmed their faith in fundamental human rights, in the dignity and worth of the human person and in the equal rights of men and women,

Considering that the Universal Declaration of Human Rights asserts the principle of nondiscrimination and proclaims that all human beings are born free and equal in dignity and rights and that everyone is entitled to all the rights and freedoms set forth therein, without distinction of any kind, including any distinction as to sex,

Taking into account the resolutions, declarations, conventions and recommendations of the United Nations and the specialized agencies designed to eliminate all forms of discrimination and to promote equal rights for men and women,

Concerned that, despite the Charter, the Universal Declaration of Human Rights, International Covenants on Human Rights and other instruments of the United Nations and the specialized agencies and despite the progress made in the matter of equality of rights, there continues to exist considerable discrimination against women,

Considering that discrimination against women is incompatible with human dignity, and with the welfare of the family and of society, prevents their participation on equal terms with men, in the political, social, economic and cultural life of their countries, and is an obstacle to the full development of the potentialities of women in the service of their countries and of humanity,

Bearing in mind the great contribution made by women to social, political, economic and cultural life and the part they play in the family and particularly in the rearing of children,

Convinced that the full and complete development of a country, the welfare of the world and the cause of peace require the maximum participation of women as well as men in all fields,

Considering that it is necessary to insure the universal recognition in law and in fact of the principle of equality of men and women,

Solemnly proclaims this Declaration:

ARTICLE 1

Discrimination against women, denying or limiting as it does their equality of rights with men, is fundamentally unjust and constitutes an offense against human dignity.

ARTICLE 2

All appropriate measures shall be taken to abolish existing laws, customs, regulations and practices which are discriminatory against women, and to establish adequate legal protection for equal rights of men and women, in particular:

(a) The principle of equality of rights shall be embodied in the constitution or otherwise guaranteed by law;

.(b) The international instruments of the United Nations and the specialized agencies relating to the elimination of discrimination against women shall be ratified or acceded to and fully implemented as soon as practicable.

ARTICLE 3

All appropriate measures shall be taken to educate public opinion and direct national aspirations toward the eradication of prejudice and the abolition of customary and all other practices which are based on the idea of the inferiority of women.

ARTICLE 4

All appropriate measures shall be taken to ensure to women on equal terms with men without any discrimination:

(a) The right to vote in all elections and be eligible for election to all publicly elected bodies;

(b) The right to vote in all public referenda;

(c) The right to hold public office and to exercise all public functions.

Such rights shall be guaranteed by legislation.

ARTICLE 5

Women shall have the same rights as men to acquire, change or retain their nationality. Marriage to an alien shall not automatically affect the nationality of the wife either by rendering her stateless or by forcing on her the nationality of her husband.

ARTICLE 6

1. Without prejudice to the safeguarding of the unity and the harmony of the family which remains the basic unit of any society, all appropriate measures, particularly legislative measures, shall be taken to insure to women, married or unmarried, equal rights with men in the field of civil law, and in particular:

(a) The right to acquire, administer and enjoy, dispose of and inherit property, including property acquired during the marriage;

(b) The right to equality in legal capacity and the exercise thereof;

(c) The same rights as men with regard to the law on the movement of persons.

2. All appropriate measures shall be taken to insure the principle of equality of status of the husband and wife, and in particular:

(a) Women shall have the same right as men to free choice of a spouse and to enter into marriage only with their free and full consent;

(b) Women shall have equal rights with men during marriage and at its dissolution. In all cases the interest of the child shall be paramount;

(c) Parents shall have equal rights and duties in matters relating to their children. In all cases the interest of the children shall be paramount.

3. Child marriage and the bethrothal of young girls before puberty shall be prohibited, and effective action, including legislation, shall be taken to specify a minimum age for marriage and to make the registration of marriages in an official registry compulsory.

ARTICLE 7

All provisions of penal codes which constitute discrimination against women shall be repealed.

ARTICLE 8

All appropriate measures, including legislation, shall be taken to combat all forms of traffic in women and exploitation of prostitution of women.

ARTICLE 9

All appropriate measures shall be taken to insure to girls and women, married or unmarried, equal rights with men in education at all levels, and in particular:

(a) Equal conditions of access to, and study in, educational institutions of all types, including universities, vocational, technical and professional schools;

(b) The same choice of curricula, the same examinations, teaching staff with qualifications of the same standard, and school premises and equipment of the same quality, whether the institutions are coeducational or not;

(c) Equal opportunities to benefit from scholarships and other study grants;

(d) Equal opportunities for access to programs of continuing education, including adult literacy programs;

(e) Access to educational information to help in insuring the health and well-being of families.

ARTICLE 10

1. All appropriate measures shall be taken to insure to women, married or unmarried, equal rights with men in the field of economic and social life, and in particular:

(a) The right without discrimination on grounds of marital status or any other grounds, to receive vocational training, to work, to free choice of profession and employment, and to professional and vocational advancement;

(b) The right to equal remuneration with men and to equality of treatment in respect of work of equal value;

(c) The right to leave with pay, retirement privileges and provision for security in respect of unemployment, sickness, old age or other incapacity to work;

(d) The right to receive family allowances on equal terms with men.

2. In order to prevent discrimination against women on account of marriage or maternity and to insure their effective right to work, measures shall be taken to prevent their dismissal in the event of marriage or maternity and to provide paid maternity leave, and the guarantee of returning to former employment, and to provide the necessary social services, including childcare facilities.

3. Measures taken to protect women in certain types of work, for reasons inherent in their physical nature, shall not be regarded as discriminatory.

ARTICLE 11

The principle of equality of rights of men and women demands implementation in all states in accordance with the principles of the United Nations Charter and of the Universal Declaration of Human Rights.

Governments, nongovernmental organizations and individuals are urged, therefore, to do all in their power to promote the implementation of the principles contained in this Declaration.

Index